de activate anxiety. simple strategies for claiming the life you've longed for.

LARISSA DE MICHIEL

De Activate Anxiety
Copyright 2022 ©Larissa De Michiel

Published by Star Label Publishing
P.O. Box 1511, Buderim, QLD, Australia
publishing@starlabel.com.au

Editing and Interior design: Rebecca Moore
Editing: David Goodwin, Mandy Chandler
Cover art: Kelly Weitz

1st Edition September, 2022
All rights reserved. No part of this publication may be reproduced in any form; stored in a retrieval system; or transmitted; or used in any other form; or by any other means without prior written permission of the publisher (except for brief quotes for the purpose of review or promotion).

All Scripture quotations unless otherwise indicated are from The Holy Bible, New International Version®, NIV® Copyright © 1973, 1978, 1984, 2011 by Biblica, Inc.™ Used by permission. All rights reserved worldwide.

Scripture quotations marked AMP are taken from the Amplified® Bible (AMP), Copyright © 2015 by The Lockman Foundation, Used by permission. www.Lockman.org.

Scripture quotations marked (NLT) are taken from the Holy Bible, New Living Translation, copyright © 1996, 2004, 2007 by Tyndale House Foundation. Used by permission of Tyndale House Publishers, Inc., Carol Stream, IL 60188. All rights reserved.

Scripture taken from the New King James Version®. Copyright © 1982 by Thomas Nelson, Inc. Used by permission. All rights reserved.

Scripture quotations taken from the New American Standard Bible®, Copyright© 1960, 1962, 1963, 1968, 1971, 1972, 1973, 1975, 1977, 1995 by The Lockman Foundation. Used by permission.

Scripture quotations marked (BSB) are taken from The Holy Bible, Berean Study Bible, BSB. Copyright ©2016, 2018 by Bible Hub. Used by Permission. All Rights Reserved Worldwide. www.berean.bible

[Scripture quotations are from] Revised Standard Version of the Bible, copyright © 1946, 1952, and 1971 National Council of the Churches of Christ in the United States of America. Used by permission. All rights reserved worldwide.

Scripture quotations marked (ESV) are from The Holy Bible, English Standard Version® (ESV®), copyright©2001 by Crossway, a publishing ministry of Good News Publishers. Used by permission. All rights reserved.

The views expressed here-in remain the sole responsibility of the author, who exempts the publisher from all liability. The author and publisher do not assume responsibility for any loss, damage, or disruption caused by the contents, errors or omissions, whether such contents, errors, or omissions result from opinion, negligence, accident, or any other cause, and hereby disclaim any and all liability to any party.

ISBN: 978-0-6453697-3-1

endorsements

This is a healthy and engaging read on anxiety. Larissa's insight, through lived experience, is like oxygen to the soul. Her open, transparent and vulnerable approach gives us the tools and most importantly the hope, that no matter where we are today, God can help us find our true north.

Pastor Ross Abraham
Chairman of International Network of Churches
Lead Pastor Elevation Church Australia

Anxiety prevents many from finishing their beautiful and unique life story. Here in her book, Larissa gives clear strategies to assist in conquering those anxieties that try to hold a person back from fulfilling their true life's purpose. Thank you, Larissa, for such a real and courageous book.

Elder Pastor Sandra Dumas
Senior Pastor of Ganggalah Church and
5 Stones Indigenous Leadership
ACC National Indigenous Initiate Leader

De Activate Anxiety is one of those books that is raw, real and packed full of revelation for the searching heart and mind. This book is a must read for all ages and will arm them with effective tools to navigate life. This is a brilliant piece of work and a wonderful tool that is going to help so many people.

Pastors Brad and Kim Otto
Senior Pastor's of COH Church, Gold Coast
ACTS National Leadership Team

If you struggle with anxiety, you will find a friend in this book. I own a few books on the subject, but this one is different. It is both a personal story, a practical resource, highly informative and deeply spiritual. I found the book profound and readable, all at the same time. Larissa shares her own mental health journey with such honesty and vulnerability, yet is highly conscious of you the reader, serving you at every step of the way. I got the strong impression that my journey and my freedom actually mattered to her. That's quite an achievement.

Vicki Simpson
Minister, conference speaker and coach
C3 SYD Church, Oxford Falls, Sydney

Larissa De Michiel has poured her life and experience into this book. She provides key ideas and strategies for overcoming anxiety based on the Bible that emphasise Spirit-filled living. Those facing similar struggles can be enriched from her healing journey learn practical strategies for their own lives.

Rev Dr Jacqueline Grey
Professor of Biblical Studies
Alphacrucis University College

Deactivate Anxiety is a brave and helpful exploration of mental health from a Christian perspective. Fully endorsing clinical best practices while highlighting the spiritual reality of a journey that so many young adults walk through. I will have a stack of these on my shelf ready to pass on to young adults that I counsel for their own well-being and freedom."

Pastor Tim Biasetto
NSW Director Youth Alive Academy
Discipleship Pastor, Horizon Church

This is a practical yet deeply personal and powerful guide that I'm sure will help many who grapple with anxiety. What I appreciate most about Larissa's book is how she has unashamedly shares her Christian faith and the critical role it has played in her mental health journey, while acknowledging the importance of having clinical support in place at the same time. The two-work hand in glove and that's such an important message."

Gemma Tognini
Award winning business owner, media personality
Opinion writer and public speaker

What a powerful and engaging book! From the moment you open the first page there is honesty, transparency and a deep rawness. This book is dense with practical activities and deep spiritual and gospel truths. Through each chapter, Larissa offers insights by being vulnerable, spiritual, and practical. For anyone reading this book because a loved one is battling anxiety, this book will offer understanding, compassion, and most of all hope! Larissa is a trusted prophetic voice in our church community, as well as a dear friend and we believe she has conveyed her heart beautifully in this book. "

Pastor's Lachlan and Tara Jones
Lead Pastors of Elevation Church, Tweed Coast

dedication

To my husband,
my Ma,
and my 'sisters'
Kristy and Melinda.

"Love makes your soul
crawl out from its hiding place."
—Zora Neale Hurston

Contents Page

chapter 1 — the starting point...1

chapter 2 — deep surrender..11

chapter 3 — knowledge unlocks power...............................27

chapter 4 — gaining altitude with gratitude.......................47

chapter 5 — meaningful mindfulness...................................61

chapter 6 — activating tender loving care..........................71

chapter 7 — let's get spiritual..85

chapter 8 — taking a stand...97

chapter 9 — access denied...109

chapter 10 — the sweetest victory......................................121

chapter 11 — the power of agreement..............................133

chapter 12 — your divine authority...................................151

chapter 13 — soul arise...163

chapter 14 — the deeper place...177

chapter 15 — the ultimate comeback................................195

bonus: your resource section...202

acknowledgements...207

about the author..209

chapter 1

the starting point

> You cannot go back and change the beginning, but you can start where you are and change the ending.
> —C.S. Lewis

Congratulations! Well done for picking up this book and taking a fresh step toward owning and dominating your anxiety. For some of you, this is the beginning of a journey; for others, this is another significant step in your healing expedition.

Anxiety and all her family members, like worry, stress, fear, and dread, are impacting us and our generation with ferocity. If you have picked up this book because you are in your own battle, you are not alone. You are part of a growing number of people who are battling issues related to mental health.

Depression and anxiety are increasingly global issues. As an example, I live in Australia, where, in 2018, one in five people suffered a mental or behavioural health issue.[1]

---
1   National Health Survey of 2017–18

Tragically, suicide claims the lives of more Australians between the ages of 15 and 44 than any other cause, and with the current state of the world, this number looks set only to increase.

Never has there been a time where learning the keys to a healthier inner life is more imperative.

If you have picked up this book because you are seeking to co-create a life that is better going forward than it has been in the past, then I believe this book is for you. If you are battling your own mental health challenges around worry, fear, stress or anxiety, and are longing for answers, I will join you in your quest to that end.[2]

This book is tailored for those dealing with anxiety, panic attacks, high stress or fear, who love Jesus or want to know Him better, and who desire to figure out the grand plan for their lives on this planet. Whether you are dealing with one or all of these issues, this book is written with you in mind.

As you read this book, my deep desire is that you will gain new insight into how to deactivate anxiety in your life. That you will discover a whole new world of managing anxiety, which at its heart is not ego centric but born of heaven. That you will learn coping strategies bathed in the

---

2   Let me say at the forefront of this journey together—if you are dealing with debilitating anxiety or panic attacks I am neither a GP nor a psychologist. If you are being crippled by your mental health, and haven't already done so, please go and see a health practitioner. I want to make sure that this book is part of a holistic healing care plan for you. I will discuss this in more detail as we move forward together.

the starting point

anointing and the presence of the Father, Son, and Holy Spirit.

This is not meant to be a 'self-help' book, but a Spirit-inspired experience with divine impartation and transformation!

The truth is we got ourselves into many of the problems we are facing, so why on earth would we think we can get ourselves out alone? After more than 20 years of walking with Jesus, I am convinced that He desires to walk alongside us, out of the messes we have made for ourselves. This book is my attempt to share with you how He got me out of my huge mess, and it is a testament to His heart for doing the same for you.

To begin this journey together, I will share more about my own mess #goodtimes. I do this in the hope that you will see some of your own story in these pages and to help you regain hope, just as I have, that life can be different— even if you are at the bottom of a pit.

safety instructions: Before we take off, I really want to share an important thought. Anyone about to head off on a journey is given safety instructions that are vital along the way. I want to make sure you are given instructions to keep you safe on this journey too, and they will be flagged with this icon.

My story includes some potentially triggering content like abuse, suicide, and other traumas. The absolute best bet, if you are triggered by anything you come across, is to talk with an expert before proceeding. I have a story to tell, but while I am a pastor with a degree in theology and 20 years' experience in pastoral care and secular coaching, I am neither a psychologist or GP. I will discuss this further in the next chapter, but from the onset, I wanted to reinforce that if you need expert help, please reach out for it. And if you aren't sure where to start, I have put together a resource chapter at the end of the book.

Let me give you a quick look at my life today. I am happy, content, living with purpose, and full of gratitude. I'm married to a fantastic man who is truly my partner in life, Lorenzo, and we have two beautiful, rambunctious girls. It is a wonderful and full season that feels like a larger divine harmony. I was on the pastoral team at Horizon Church in Sydney from 2004 until 2020, have been a credentialed pastor since 2009, and have been in Christian ministry since 1998. Our family now lives on the beautiful Tweed Coast of NSW Australia and serving the local church and community.

However, my life has NOT always been flourishing, either internally or externally. Like many, I had a broken and dysfunctional upbringing. My early years were a mixed bag—at times dark, at other times filled with opportunities and privilege.

Both my parents were highly regarded academics

and influential in their respective fields. Although retired, my mother is still an Emeritus Professor whose expertise is internationally sought after, while my father was an outstanding scholar, well known in education circles and held significant education roles nationally up until his death in 2016. My parents were and are, inspirations to me on so many levels with their vocational achievements. They've both authored a multitude of books and journal articles, been recognised with a plethora of awards in their respective fields, sat on national boards, were sought after nationally and internationally as speakers, and ultimately influenced the multitudes. Their career success is truly breathtaking and admirable.

So, it is not surprising they championed high achievement in my life. I learnt that being a woman meant I was strong and capable—not weak and needy. They taught me to walk with confidence (even if I had to "fake it 'til I made it"), to love the excitement of competition, to treat the garbage woman with the same respect as I would the CEO, and to be a contributor to my community. These values and others they taught me are ones I am deeply grateful for, as they have served me well. My mother in particular, has been a significant role model in how to lead with fairness, humour, and strength.

I have learnt from them both and have much to be grateful for in retrospect and reflection. There is genuine honour in my heart today for my parents. However, as a 21-year-old, I had neither retrospect nor reflection. I did not possess the substance of grace and forgiveness living in my soul to extend to their weakness as I do today. What I did have at 21 was a mountain of undealt with pain and destructive coping patterns as a result of the darker parts of my childhood.

I was working out deep abandonment, stemming from being sent away very unexpectantly to boarding school at the age of 12 after my parents divorced. I was also experiencing the repercussions of childhood abuse, which included the sexual misconduct of a significant adult in my family. I would later discover that I had been in an active, and what I thought was a loving, relationship with this paedophile for many years. This defiled relationship caused so much damage in my life.

Let me just make this very clear, though. God is bigger than an abuser, and His love is stronger than any corrupt touch.

I will expand on this toward the end of the book when we talk about dealing with the root causes of anxiety. It is enough to say here that, by the age of 21, I was in a world of hurt and couldn't find my way out. Thank God that Jesus found me!

My conversion was rather radical. At the time of my salvation experience, I was a heavy drug user which was compounded by some severe mental health issues (many of which were not diagnosed until over a decade later). I

the starting point

battled a type of intense anxiety disorder in which you fear and avoid places or situations that might cause you to feel trapped, helpless or embarrassed. This meant I couldn't cope with situations like public transport, movie theatres or going anywhere with people I didn't know. Every time I needed to leave my house it would trigger a panic attack.

I would self-medicate with marijuana, other illicit drugs, and alcohol to build up the courage to walk out the front door—which I gradually did less and less, and never without being highly inebriated. I was drinking something, sniffing something or smoking something from the moment I woke up until the time I passed out in bed at night. This was my day, every day. So, by the time God revealed himself to me, it's fair to say that, even though I was still young, I had made a total mess of my life and had no way out.

I had isolated myself from my family and friends and was living 40 kms out of town in a place called Devils Pinch. I couldn't have scripted this name any better! It was an accurate description of my location, as true in geography as it was in the spiritual. I was lost, caught in a cycle of drugs, and trapped in a serious situation with some dangerous people.

I had nothing to offer God when I met Jesus other than brokenness, wickedness, and filth. Yet, He still called me, forgave me, and filled me with His Spirit.

Which is the grace available to us all, isn't it? He did not call me when I was well, He called me at the height of my illness and said, "Yep, you're my girl." It still amazes me to this day, causing deep emotions of gratitude as I think back to those times. He wants to do the same thing for us all. While we are still messed up, broken, not perfect—God wants to tell us, "Yep, son, daughter, I love you just the way you are." And this love doesn't stop once we are Christians; it's a never-ending pull of God to draw us back, and back again, to His road of life.

> Brothers and sisters think of what you were when you were called. Not many of you were wise by human standards; not many were influential; not many were of noble birth. But God chose the foolish things of the world to shame the wise; God chose the weak things of the world to shame the strong. God chose the lowly things of this world and the despised things—and the things that are not—to nullify the things that are, so that no one may boast before him.
> —1 Corinthians 1:26–29

If you're reading this, and feeling like life is all messed up, let me tell you God is into restoration, healing, and fixing things up. Not just once or twice or three times, but repeatedly—over and over and over again. It is His nature to take you just as you are and create something remarkable because of His love for you. If you aren't in a huge mess, but are dealing with your own stresses or fears, He can take that too and turn it around. Big or small, complex or seemingly simple, God is here for you right now as you read this book, wanting to take your life as it is—and guide you forward.

I mentioned at the beginning of this chapter that this book isn't intended to be a self-help manual for your life. The absolute intent of these words you are reading is that they serve as an encounter with your God, your Creator—who knows you better than you know yourself. Knowing Him and calling on Him are the beginning of your way out.

Throughout this book, I will encourage you to pray to God, to become aware of Him in these pages, and to turn your attention toward Him. You can use the words I have written down in the prayer below, or you can use your own. They are simply a prompt to help keep Him front and centre in this journey. I'd love for you to do that now. Take some time to connect with Jesus. Perhaps put on some worship music or take out your journal and give yourself some time to sit, be still, and pray.

 "Lord Jesus, I give You my life afresh just as it is. I turn toward You with my heart open again and ask You to lead me forward. I want You to be front and centre in this journey of healing and freedom. Help me hear Your voice and feel Your presence as I read the pages of this book. Amen."

HIGHLIGHTS

- **Congratulations!** Well done for picking up this book and making a fresh step toward owning and dominating your anxiety.

- This book is tailored for those dealing with anxiety, panic attacks, high stress, and fear—or those wanting to support someone dealing with any of these—and who love Jesus and desire to figure out His grand plan on this planet.

- This is not meant to be a 'self-help' book, but a Holy Spirit-inspired experience with divine impartation!

- Spend time connecting with your heavenly Father today.

- Would you like to join myself and others in deactivate anxiety in person? You're welcome to join the private Facebook group De Activate Anxiety. Look for De Activate Anxiety in your search engine on Facebook or fill in the following link: https://www.facebook.com/groups/141652122113692/

chapter 2

deep surrender

As we journey, you will find that I primarily speak about anxiety and panic attacks—because that has been my battle. However, for you, it might be deep worry, it might be intense stress, or it might be uncontrollable fear. Or perhaps, you are reading this book to better understand what a loved one is going through. Whatever you or your loved one is facing, in my opinion the symptoms are all related. So, when you hear me talk about my panic attacks, I just want you to translate that to whatever it is that you are dealing with. The deactivation tools that I share in this book will work on them too.

✎ **exercise:** Along the way, there will be opportunity for you to do some exercises and activations. I'd love us to engage in one now. Can you remember the first time you experienced anxiety at a level that affected you deeply? I don't want you to concentrate on the event, I just want you to reflect on when you can first remember anxiety becoming part of your life.

✈ **safety instructions:** This chapter touches on abuse and self-harm. If you are struggling with thoughts of self-harm, you must reach out for help. Please go to a health professional—ring up now and make an appointment. Call a friend or family member and tell them you are struggling. Call another community support group such as the mental health clinic at your local hospital and tell your story. Telling people is the first step, and if you need guidance, there are lots of resources for help at the end of the book.

The first time I remember experiencing intense panic was when I was 11 years-old at my dad's wedding to his second wife. It was a highly stressful event for me as my parents had only separated a year earlier, and I was still coming to terms with the fact that they were not getting back together. There were other factors at play—My relationship with my dad was very convoluted and I was about to be sent to boarding school in my *own hometown*.

There were also some other very complex family dynamics at work, including the sexual molestation by an adult in our family's world. The wedding day seemed to compound all these realities, and then, to add more pressure, the occasion was being televised for the local news as my dad was running for a seat in a local election.

As the music began, and I stood at the aisle about to walk down in my pretty flower girl dress, it all came crashing down on me—the deep grief for the life I had lost. In front of the cameras, and in front of all our friends, I cried uncontrollably. It's fair to say the glass of champagne I'd been given just prior to this moment probably didn't help me to control my emotions. I was a total mess, and I've never felt embarrassment like it.

I remember thinking, "Why can't I stop crying? Pull it together, you are embarrassing yourself." But the tears kept coming, and what felt like looks of disdain and judgment from the guests at the wedding burnt deep.

To my horror, I was finally escorted out of the wedding by one of Dad's groomsmen. I felt weak, embarrassed, and deeply shamed about who I was. I remember everything becoming very dark and feeling very alone. It was the first time in my life I felt totally out of control, and I vowed never to feel that way again. This was, however, only the beginning of what became a lifestyle of ever-increasing fear, anxiety, and panic.

I look back today at that little girl, and my compassion for her is deep.

I wish I could have held her and told her she was brave and magnificent. In fact, over the years, I have done just that, and I would encourage you to view your childhood through the same lens of compassion. However, I didn't receive compassion that day, and a seed of shame and fear was sown into my core, and a severe personal fracture took place.

Up until this event, I had been known by the name 'Lara'. However, during this season of my life, I took on my more formal name 'Larissa' and demanded everyone make the change. The motivation for this shift was deep self-loathing connected to all that had happened to 'Lara' during this time. It was also the beginning of a lie about what was really going on for me, and the start of a public persona that concealed my mental health challenges.

During my teenage years, my mental health was a mess. By year 11 I had been 'asked to leave' by the principal of the boarding school and was now attending a local high school and living back at home. I would go to school and pretend things were normal, and then come home each afternoon and lie on my bed and cry for hours. I began drinking and taking drugs to suffocate the internal chaos and anxiety with ever increasing frequency, until I was 21 and encountered Jesus. Unfortunately, due to the situation I was in, coming to Christ didn't remove the life of fear.

I wish my story was different, but even as a born-again and Spirit-filled Christian pastor, I would still have to deal with panic attacks, high fear, and anxiety. In truth, there are still experiences today that draw me into a panic cycle. However, the difference is that I now have the tools (the ones that I'm going to share with you) to bring myself back out when fear tries to take a hold.

During my twenties and thirties, I lived with the secret shame of not being able to 'cure' my mental health, and the embarrassment of thinking I must have lacked faith. I thought there must have been something wrong with me because my worldview at the time didn't allow for the tension between Christ's victory on the Cross and human suffering. I am so thankful my theology has come to a deeper understanding today.

Mental health still has a stigma in our society and even more so in the church. I remember being plagued with the thought, "What sort of Christian am I if I can't fix this issue in my life?" Perhaps you have had similar thoughts that Christians shouldn't struggle with mental health issues. If so, then let me be very clear: *that is a lie from the pit.* Are you less a Christian if you suffer with cancer, diabetes or the flu? Of course not! Part of the reason that I wanted to write this book is to contribute to removing this stigma by addressing some of the unhelpful judgements around mental health in the church.

Does God want you to find total freedom and healing? Of course. However, this is a process, which means there will be parts of that journey where you love God and struggle with your mental health <u>at the same time</u>!

I do think that healing can be instantaneous, and that God does choose to move miraculously in particular struggles. For example, I know when I met Jesus, I was radically delivered from drugs—almost in a single moment.

But with regard to the panic attacks and high fear and anxiety, the transformation was not instantaneous for me. How I wished, prayed, and fasted that it would be! It has instead been a process where things got worse before I experienced victory, and a journey that I've discovered still requires faith.

It could be argued that the road of long suffering requires us to show a greater faith than if we had been healed before that road even began.

I experienced almost three decades of panic attacks and crippling anxiety before I found transformation, new hope, and new ways of managing my stress. However, once I started actioning these strategies, I began to experience results. These strategies that I will share in this book are simple, and if you commit to them, I believe they will revolutionise your life as they have mine. These tools have been birthed from the darkest chapter of my life, and this book contains the gold I gained from a time where I hit rock bottom after decades of silent struggle.

It is always darkest before the dawn.

For my entire adult life, the level of my anxiety has been a secret from most of the people in my world. Yet, at the age of 29, I could not pretend there weren't major problems any longer. My anxiety finally erupted with an uncontrollable force that left me with my first nervous breakdown.

A bunch of things were going on at the time. I was working nights at a youth refuge and days at my church. I had some family stress that was surfacing, and I was starting to deal with sexual abuse from my childhood. One shift at the refuge, a young teenage boy violently pulled a knife on me. Later that night, as I was lying in bed, a very familiar feeling of aloneness, fear, and anxiety overtook me. It became so intense that I threw up, and it flung me into a spiral of uncontrolled emotions which I didn't emerge from for four months.

During those months, I hardly ate or slept. I was trapped in a panic cycle that had no end—like falling down a hole with no bottom. Looking back, I think the biggest source of trauma was not knowing why it was happening, what was happening or when it would end. I began having tormenting thoughts and invasive urges around suicide, and I felt like I was being subjected to an assault which I had no idea how to combat. I will be forever grateful to my flatmates at the time, Kristy Mills and Jacqui Grey, who are more like sisters and carried me through when I was drowning.

I sought treatment; I went on medication. I stopped working at the refuge, and I completely changed my life in terms of the pace I was living. I slowly regained my sanity but ultimately, I had no real idea what had happened to me or how it was I had eventually come back into my right mind.

Going forward, I started to rebuild. But in the background, there was always an underlying beat, a constant rumbling of fear that, in time, when I least expected it, another episode would 'get me'. Every time I experienced a panic attack, I thought I was falling back into the extremes I had experienced when I was 29. To compensate, my life and its experiences grew smaller and smaller as I tried to control any possible onset.

I never went on public transport—I wouldn't go anywhere I felt I was going to be trapped. And I always had to sit on the aisle seat when I went to movies. I had to be facing the door in a restaurant, and I wouldn't travel anywhere unless I could drive myself. Looking back, I can see every main event of my life for the next decade was accompanied by panic and fear.

A large part of my own wedding was spent huddled in a foetal position in a hidden room, unable to breathe and throwing up from uncontrolled anxiety. How grateful I am for a husband who locked himself in there with me, missing out on all the food and festivities of our wedding to just be with me in my panic.

I loved the Lord, and there was strength in my life. I was a pastor, and I contributed to my church in many ways—as long as there was routine, and a level of familiarity and control. If those elements were present, I was fine; I was strong; I was even dynamic. But, faced with a situation where they were absent, I couldn't cope, and panic would overtake me—this was something that happened often.

I remember being asked to preach and needing two weeks of mental preparation to manage the onslaught of panic. It was often too much, and I would end up declining the invitation. I remember being asked to run or be involved in mission trips on more than one occasion, and with every opportunity, I had an excuse why I couldn't go.

So, that's where I was when my life came crashing to a halt in my late thirties. By this stage, I was married and had just given birth to my first child. Anyone who has had kids knows that a newborn couldn't care less about your routine, coping strategies or level of control.

Even before having a baby, my life was already a bubbling cauldron. My ministry was under some serious strain at that stage—as was my marriage. I had also recently had a miscarriage at 12 weeks, which meant the lead up to the birth carried a degree of apprehension, and (like a constant foul smell in my life) I was once again attempting to unravel some deep issues relating to childhood sexual abuse.

Anxiety was high when my first baby was introduced to my life. After three weeks with the newborn, plus the other stressors in the forefront of my life, I think my internal workings just gave in. I did not have the coping strategies for the life I was in. I gazed upon this beautiful baby girl, fully dependant on me, and when I looked inside, I just knew I didn't have the capacity to be available for her in the way she deserved. I was completely broken.

My sanity and centredness had left me, and in their place, was the highest level of panic and fear I had ever experienced in my life. I have no words that could describe to you what the next year of my life would be like. To look at my life and know that I had lost my mind was the scariest reality I have ever faced. I couldn't control my thoughts, and the darkness I was in was a real place I couldn't escape.

I remember collapsing in my husband's arms and finally admitting something was very wrong. He loved, and loves me dearly, but he would be the first to tell you, he felt very helpless. My mum had just retired, and after speaking with Lorenzo, it was decided she would come and live with us. We didn't realise it would become an eight month on-and-off arrangement.

I am so very grateful for her! There is no doubt in any of our minds that without her, I would have been hospitalised for a good length of time—or worse. I remember going to the local hospital and being admitted as an outpatient in the mental health ward. I would go to see the psychiatrist and be demoralised and humbled as I waited in the waiting room. I would look at these other people who were suffering, and I could see the reality of my situation through their eyes.

Some of these patients knew me as a local church pastor and would ask for prayer. I couldn't pray for myself, let alone someone else, I was utterly broken. But I couldn't bring myself to admit that I was there for my own struggles and would play along with the assumption I was there for a pastoral visit. In time, the nurses saw what was happening, and would whisk me away the moment I arrived. I am grateful for their kindness.

Let me just say, being at the local mental health ward in a public hospital was necessary, but it did little for my sense of self-worth. It was so clinical and sterile, and I personally hated every visit—but I needed it. I am thankful for a country that has the healthcare system that we do, but I also felt demoralised.

I tried different medications while experiencing psychotic reactions. Again, I couldn't eat, sleep, think, hold a conversation or be around anyone, bar a few trusted people. I forgot how to drive, cook, and at times, how to say my own name. I would throw up continually. I couldn't stand noise, and I was just a complete mess. To lose your mind is a horrendous experience—I know no other way to explain it.

I remember at the height of it, I'd gone for a walk on my own and everything slowed down to an eerie pace. Nothing I did helped, I couldn't stop the panic and fear drilling through my body 24 hours a day, seven days a week. There was no reprieve, I was helpless. As I saw a truck driving toward me, I waited to cross at the lights. A feeling of clarity filled my mind, and I had this sensation, almost like a premonition, that I could cure it all if I just stepped out in front of the oncoming vehicle.

I saw myself in my mind being struck by the truck, and

I remember thinking how much better off everyone would be. I felt like a burden to those I loved and was crushed by the thought of my daughter having to grow up with a mother that loved her desperately but couldn't get her mind right. It would be so easy to fix it all, I thought. In that moment, I saw with complete clarity how to solve this debilitating problem—the problem that was me. I started to walk out but, as I looked up and saw the driver, my mind flashed with an image of his family. In a single second, I saw a movie play out showing his life after taking mine, and it stopped me—but it didn't heal me.

After this experience, I was defeated and had come to the end of my strength. I'd done everything I knew to do for almost two decades to fix this, and I had been dealing with the symptoms since I was that 11-year-old girl at my father's wedding. I'd answered every altar call, was fully committed to the journey of inner healing, loved God, and had been in ministry for about 15 years.

I had listened to podcasts, tried medication, and seen counsellors, psychologists, and psychiatrists. And yet, here I was, still filled with panic and anxiety, and at a complete loss as to how to get better. I just remember thinking, "I give up." To be honest though, the language at the time was probably far more colourful.

Then I felt the whisper of the Holy Spirit. As He so beautifully does when He rebukes us, He kindly said, "That's right my daughter, *you* have done everything you can. Now let *Me* guide you." It was like everything became very clear.

Ever had those moments when you sense God talking to you, and in a moment, His words change everything?

I thought, "You're right!" Which He is, obviously, because He's God! I thought, *I have* done everything. *I have* been to every altar call. *I have* gone and sought counselling. *I have* tried different medications. *I had* taken control of the healing and the responsibility of fixing the problem. But what I needed to do was surrender it over to God completely and give Him full control.

This was the turning point in my life in dealing with anxiety and learning to deactivate it.

In that moment, I realised that I had been taking the driver's seat in my healing, when what I needed to do was surrender that position of control to God and move on over. I had no way of fixing things on my own. I needed to hand them over to Jesus and trust that the Cross, that great exchange of His life for mine, was enough. I needed to trust that He could lead me forward if I was prepared to follow.

You may have already done that, but I'd like to invite you, as we commence this journey together, to bring the anxiety—or whatever it is that brought you to this book—and freshly surrender the issues you are facing to Jesus. Be open to Him guiding the healing, the transformation, and the victory into your life. Are you up for it? It is where we start.

I have learnt keys and strategies and tools that have changed the game when it comes to panic attacks, and I'm going to share them all with you. But it all starts with surrendering your life to Jesus afresh.

> Cast all your anxiety on him because he cares for you.
> —1 Peter 5:7

"Father, thank you for bringing us to this spot. We declare You are Emmanuel, God in the midst of us. We believe that You loved us so much that You sent Your Son to die on the Cross. You did this to show us that You want to take our lives just as they are and bear our pain and anxieties. We believe that You can make a way out of our anxious lives, even though we may not be able to see it ourselves yet.

Show us the path of life, and Holy Spirit, we ask that You come afresh into our hearts today. We breathe You in; we love You. Please anoint us each time we come to read the pages in this book. Help us to hear what it is we need to hear for our own personal breakthroughs. In Jesus' name, Amen."

HIGHLIGHTS

- I had nothing to offer God when I met Jesus other than brokenness, wickedness, and filth. Yet He still called me, forgave me, and filled me with His Spirit, which is the grace available to us all, isn't it?

- I am now pretty awesome ☺, but I wasn't always as content. If you want to hear some of what really messed me up, and what brought me to writing this book, then you might like to go back and read this chapter.

- Can I just reinforce once more, if you are dealing with debilitating anxiety or panic, please go and see a health professional? Make sure that this book is part of a holistic care plan for you. I am not a doctor; I am just sharing my own story. If you are struggling, then reach out for professional help. That is the brave next step for you. There are a bunch of excellent resources for your support in the resources chapter at the end of this book.

- The key is the power of surrendering your life to Jesus—just as it is. Your story needs to be aligned with His story for you, and that can only happen when we invite Him into the guts of our troubles.

chapter 3

knowledge unlocks power

> And His name will be called Wonderful Counsellor, Mighty God, Eternal Father, Prince of Peace.
> —Isaiah 9:6 (NASB)

It is both wonderful and reassuring to me that Jesus is known as the Prince of Peace. We are not trying to obtain just a feeling or an absence of anxiety. Instead, we are seeking the person of Jesus. This is my prayer for you as you read this book, that you integrate the deepest parts of who you are with our Wonderful Counsellor, Mighty God, Eternal Father and **Prince of Peace**.

It is this relationship that brings the true peace which surpasses all understanding. It's the kind of peace that changes who we are and how we engage with the world, and it is available to us all. I know from my own life, I have experienced deep levels of peace and wellness, not only from activating the tools that I am going to be sharing with you in this book, but ultimately, because of my connection with Jesus. Every tool that I share in the following chapters is founded on a living, dynamic, and interconnected bond with Him.

To not have that relationship is to have the tools but be disconnected from the power source.

Okay, with the foundations laid, and with you knowing a little more about what led me to writing this book, let's dive into the first tool for deactivating anxiety. This tool is the acquiring of knowledge—because knowledge unlocks power.

I think when the Bible tells us in Hosea 4:6 that the people of God were perishing through a lack of knowledge, this is also true for how we manage anxiety in our lives. If we can understand what is happening inside of us during periods of high stress, then the power of overcoming this unknown can help to deactivate the anxiety, while also giving us traction in mastering and managing it.

I remember the light bulb moment when I first had someone explain to me what was happening to me during a panic attack. It was during the first of my breakdowns, and I was seeing a psychologist. She explained the internal process of anxiety in my body, and what had been an unknown started to make sense. I felt less insane because the knowledge she was giving me made my experiences explainable. As I received more information, I had more ammunition to manage the anxiety and make better decisions moving forward. My hope is this will be the case for you too.

To help in this task, I'd like to start by introducing you to the *Flow of Stress*. Take a look at the graphic below.

Flow of Stress

Since I am definitely not a psychologist, let me explain in laymen's terms what happens in our bodies when we experience anxiety. The onset of any anxious experience starts with what is known as a trigger. This can be internal, like you are more prone to anxiety when your heart beats faster or when something you do triggers a memory.

Triggers can also be set off externally, for example, by certain environments or people. Whether the stimuli are internal or external or both, the result is the same. Something acts as an activation or trigger causing our brains to sound warning signals that say, "Danger".

In more technical terms, when you are triggered, a message is passed to your brain, activating the limbic system and the thalamus.

> The limbic system is where emotions evolve, and the thalamus serves as the switch board determining what to do with the incoming messages. This is when the hypothalamus comes into play, which is the part of the brain that 'sounds the alarm'.[3]

---
3   Greenberg, J.R Comprehensive Stress Management Tenth Edition, University of Maryland (McGraw - Hill Companies Inc, New York, 2008) page 23

Looking back, I can now see there were emotional connections to my triggers or perceived realities. My triggers were connected to anything I perceived as being experiences that would trap me or leave me feeling out of control. Anything where I was going to feel vulnerable, exposed or uncomfortable were all triggers for me.

You may have already noticed a key to deactivating anxiety, and that is to change our perception. I wonder what the triggers and the connections are for you? What are the stressors that cause you to experience anxiety and panic?

Sometimes, we think our triggers are not that bad, or that we don't have many. However, if we start to ponder the things that we **don't do** in order to eliminate a cause of anxiety, we see that actually there may be many triggers in our world; we are just choosing to avoid them.

For example, I never caught public transport. I had simply removed this experience and trigger from my life. I wasn't experiencing stress related to it because I wasn't exposing myself to it. I'd like you to have a think through the things that trigger you, both in your day-to-day life and all those things which you may have removed.

When you have an idea of what sets you off, then the next step is to become curious as to why it triggers you. What is it you have perceived about this event that is causing the anxious reaction? What do you tell yourself about why you avoid this activity? What is happening at a deeper level in you, and what could be an alternate perception?

Triggers are actually our friends if we let them be. Any of my friends will tell you that when they are going through something tough, I will always ask them, "What is being triggered in you?" When we start to dialogue around what triggers us, internally as well as externally, we are actually identifying places in our souls that need the grace and healing of God. To have that kind of relationship with yourself, that ability to identify triggers, is a gift God gives to us to help us grow, mature, and find greater freedom. But more on being able to engage in this later.

After we get triggered, and an alarm sounds in our brain, what happens next? Our bodies are activated, and chemicals are pumped into our systems, which correlate with these warning signals.

Our bodies, in turn, have physical and emotional reactions to the release of these chemicals. For example, your muscles tense up, your heart starts to race, your blood pressure increases, your mouth gets dry, and you start to sweat. Perhaps, you experience problems with your stomach or your bowels, grind your teeth or get tension headaches. Along with these physical reactions, there are emotional responses that occur that are related to imaginations of doom, defeat, and even death.

However, these responses are just the beginning of the consequences of high stress and anxiety in someone's life. Dr Caroline Leaf is a world-renowned cognitive neuroscientist who suggests that **75-95% of complaints** around mental and physical illnesses come from what she classifies as toxic thinking.[4] She also proposes (as do many other experts) that unresolved stress and anxiety are the cause of many modern diseases. Stress is linked to obesity, cancer, ulcers, bowel diseases, migraines, problems with skin and hair, menstrual distress, lower immunity, allergies, arthritis, and a load of other issues.[5]

Dealing with anxiety is not only good for wellbeing, but it is potentially going to save a whole lot of physical consequences too.

If we factor the results of unresolved stress into the equation, we can now evolve our understanding of the *Flow of Stress*. See graphic below:

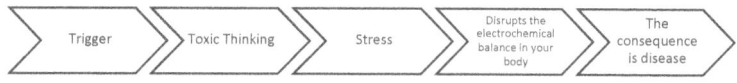

✎ **Why not take some time now, in light of this,** to think through your own Flow of Stress and fill in the table on the next page?

---

4   p37-38 Leaf, C.M., *Switch On Your Brain: The Key to Peak Happiness, Thinking, and Health*. 2013, Baker Books, Grand Rapids, Michigan
5   Greenberg, J.R Comprehensive Stress Management Tenth Edition, University of Maryland (McGraw - Hill Companies Inc, New York, 2008) page 38-55

knowledge unlocks power

Trigger Situations that cause you stress?	Toxic Thinking What is your perception of the event that is causing the stress?	Stress Response What are your physical/emotional responses to this?	Consequence List all the consequences, all the pain points of this cycle?
Going to work	Feel like I am trapped behind the reception counter	Heart races, breathing quickly, and hyperventilating. I think things like "I don't have time to function". I start to feel lightheaded.	I find work hard and unenjoyable. When I am at work, I don't do my best because I feel horrible. I get headaches.

Now, I would like you to engage with alternate ways of perceiving these triggers. Take some time to fill in the following table.

Trigger Situations that are causing you stress?	Alternate Perception What is another perception of the event that is a healthier thinking pattern?	Consequence List all the consequences that may come from holding this new perception?
Going to work	I am behind the reception counter, and I am safe. I am brave for taking steps outside my comfort zone.	Work will become more enjoyable. I will feel pride in myself and personal compassion rather than hatred and fear.

knowledge unlocks power

I have introduced to you this new idea of tracking your *Flow of Stress* because I want you to see that, when unresolved, this flow can actually become a cycle. We will refer to this next idea as a *Cycle of Anxiety*.

This is what happens when the chemicals that shout, "danger" build up in our bodies and actually **become our triggers**. The alarm bells in our minds start malfunctioning, and the anxiety becomes another trigger.

The chemicals of stress are released into the body, and in turn, the body sends messages back to the brain to inform it that there is danger. Consequently, the brain then sends out more danger messages to the body—and so the cycle continues, creating a *Cycle of Anxiety*. You'll find a visual of this cycle below:

Cycle of Anxiety

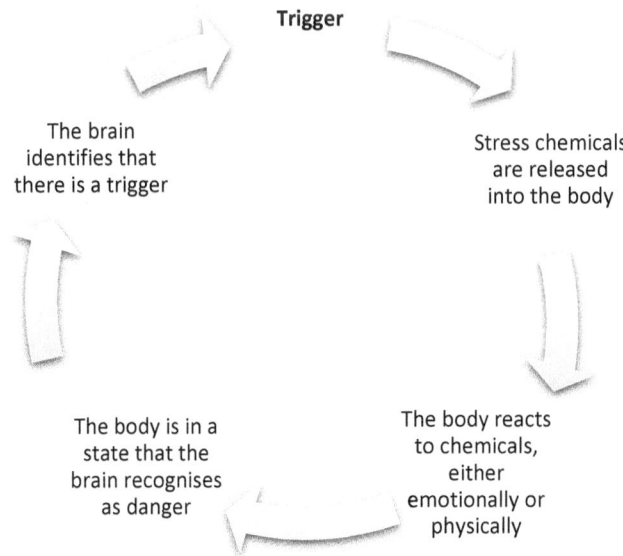

I first came to understand this when I was doing a Degree in Social Work (which I have yet to complete, mind you). I remember thinking, **"I need to learn to deactivate that cycle in my body."** Who knew that a seed had been planted, and that, a decade later, I would be writing a book about it!

Over the coming chapters, we will be looking at how to put roadblocks and detours into this *Cycle of Anxiety*. To do that and complete laying the foundation in this chapter, I will need to introduce you to one more piece of the puzzle. This is the idea of the brain having two states of being: *Protect* and *Pleasure*.

The first state of the mind or being I refer to is *Protect*. This is the state we are in when we are in the *Flow of Stress* and/or a *Cycle of Anxiety*. Stress hormones, such as adrenalin and cortisol, are pumped through our bodies because the warning bells have gone off. This is also known as an acute stress response. Being in this state of mind called *Protect* carries ideas like 'life is unsafe', 'I am not ok', 'danger', 'protect yourself' or 'stand your ground and fight'. This is where our fight or flight response kicks in, and it is the state we have been looking at until this point.

Alternatively, we can be in a state of *Pleasure*. This position comes about as the consequence of a host of fantastic endorphins being released into the body. This state carries ideas like 'I am ok' and 'things are good', and we feel safe to explore, to learn, to love, and to grow. This is the state of the mind that induces rest, healing, detoxification, and regeneration.[6]

Now it is important to understand that while our brains can alternate between these two states of being, **they can't exist simultaneously in both states.** Our minds can alternate and interchange, but at any given moment, we are either in a state of *Protect* or *Pleasure*.

To help visualise this idea of two different states of being, take a look at the simple diagram below.

Storehouse of the Mind

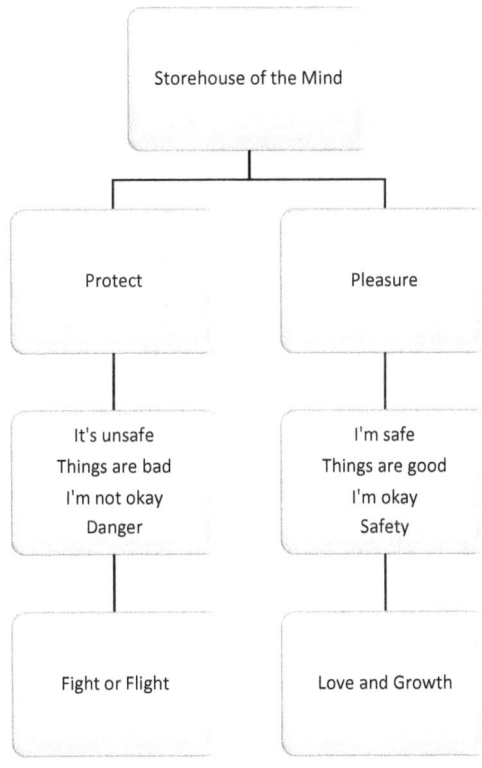

---

6   https://www.thesuppersprograms.org/content/fight-or-flight-vs-rest-and-digest 18.09.2020

Now, I have to come clean about something: it's not the aim of this book to completely eliminate the state of *Protect* from your life. Why not? Because, in the right context, being in *Protect* is imperative for your safety. If managed well, being in *Protect* is actually vital.

"No!" I hear you say. "I don't want this anxiety ever. Why would I ever want it?"

I am glad you asked.

Let's say you are going to walk out on the road, and a car is coming. You don't want to be in a state of *Pleasure* where everything seems to be okay as the car moves at speed toward you. If you weren't thrown into a state of *Protect* there is a high chance you are going to get run over, right? What about a son or daughter who is going out for the first time at night alone? Surely, we want to have cultivated a healthy understanding of their alarm system if the moment comes where they are in danger?

There are many examples of times when we want to be in the state of *Protect*, and where it is helpful. Life has real and present dangers, and we need to be able to respond appropriately. The key is to have a healthy and functional alarm system.

What happens when that alarm bell starts ringing out of control? What happens when *Protect* chemicals are constantly being pumped through our bodies? When we are triggered often or are unable to manage the triggers that life brings?

When this happens, we suffer and experience consequences such as disease. We do not want to live in a permanent or even semi-permanent state of *Protect* for long periods. We must learn to deactivate the state of *Protect* when it is not serving us.

You have come to this book because you want to learn how to deactivate your state of *Protect*.

Okay, so we have had a look at this idea of being in a *Protect* state, what about this other state of the mind called *Pleasure*? It sounds a lot more fun, doesn't it? The *Pleasure* state is all about being immersed in feelings and thoughts of enjoyment and in centredness. It is the best state to be in if, for example, you want to retain knowledge and learn.

That is why, for instance, it is very difficult to absorb information if you are in a state of heightened stress. It's why it is so difficult for kids at school to succeed academically when they are going through difficult times. If they are in a state of *Protect*, it becomes even more difficult to gather information or to be creative and curious. This is why it is so important to engage in play, and other pleasure inducing activities.

I am convinced more humour is needed in classrooms. In fact, humour and play in their appropriate forms are needed across all educational platforms, including the pulpit. I think it is a fair comment to make, then, that many of our kids (and perhaps even ourselves) have been labelled as lacking intelligence, centredness or creativity when in fact, we just aren't in the right state of mind (*Pleasure*).

Let me repeat my point because it is the basis for this book, and the **entire point** of this chapter! **You cannot exist simultaneously in both *Protect* and *Pleasure*.** You can't be pumping out 'fight or flight' messages from your brain while also producing messages of 'wellness'. We can't be highly anxious and be restful or, in the same moment say, "I'm NOT okay," and "I AM okay."

This, my friends, is the exciting news! This gives us a brilliant strategy to overcome anxiety, and also, a great idea for a book! **We can deactivate the state of *Protect* by releasing *Pleasure* messaging from our brain into our system.** That is why *Pleasure* inducing circuit breakers are imperative for the task of deactivating anxiety, and why, over the next few chapters, we will look at different tools to do just that.

When the cycle of panic and anxiety is in full swing, when the chemicals of *Protect* are being pumped out through your body, the way to move out of that state is to inject *Pleasure* into the cycle.

To put it simply, my anxiety battles were with *Flows of Stress* that turned into *Cycles of Anxiety*. Once I could see that, I realised that my whole life had become one trigger after another. Experience after experience bathed in performance anxiety, fear of rejection, worry that I would be out of control, and panic that I'd let someone down. I'd created a life where I was always trying to achieve and make people happy. Life was one big *Cycle of Anxiety*.

When I received this knowledge, it unlocked power.

I began to intentionally insert *Pleasure*-inducing activities into my days and weeks. I realised I needed to give myself permission to do this for the sake of my sanity. I could see it was now imperative that I start to practice the state of *Pleasure* because my body was desperately out of practice, and dangerously in need of it. Once I understood what was going on inside me, I made a decision to make it a priority to learn how to incorporate experiences into my life that naturally produced feelings of being okay and relaxed.

I started doing things I remembered I had liked when I was a kid. I went swimming, made time to jump in a sauna, got outside and took my baby for a walk, and soaked up the sun. When it rained, I stopped and watched the storm. I drank my coffee slowly, enjoying the taste, and watched lots of comedies. I made a list of things that made me smile, and I found a way to start enjoying my life. It didn't instantaneously fix me, there was much more to be done to deactivate the *Cycle of Anxiety*. What it did, was start a journey of transformation. Will you give yourself permission to do the same?

✎ **What I would like you to do is to start to think** of your *Pleasure*-inducing activities. What are things that create a sense of pleasure, a sense of safety, a sense of "I am okay"? It could be things like getting a hug from your husband or your kids. It could be reading a book, going to the beach or going for a walk. It could even be sex (if you're married, says the pastor in me).

What are things you can think of or reflect on that make you smile? In times when life doesn't afford me the time to walk on a beach, I think back to wonderful memories. What do you do to create those "I'm okay" pleasure inducing chemicals? Please note, there are things we can do that induce pleasure healthily—and not so healthily. Choose activities that are a win for you and not harmful.

If you have a long list of things that you can do that create a state of *Pleasure*, you have just created a bunch of beginner steps to 'circuit break' a lifestyle of anxiety. Start thinking about your *Pleasure*-creating activities. Begin a list and be inventive. Then, intentionally insert these things wherever you can throughout your day, either with frequent thoughts or intentional actions.

knowledge unlocks power

Here are some ideas to help you get the list started:

- Watching funny movies
- Going to the ocean
- Painting, reading or writing
- Infrared Sauna - research the benefits and thank me later.
- Sabbath keeping - the benefits are life changing.
- Going to the gym
- Imagination
- Dancing
- Getting out into nature
- Praying and worshiping
- Listening to podcasts
- Enjoying intimate time with husband or wife
- Having a hug
- Bath
- Massages
- Being with animals.

HIGHLIGHTS

- Flow of Stress

- When anxiety in the body itself becomes the trigger, we find ourselves in a *Cycle of Anxiety*.

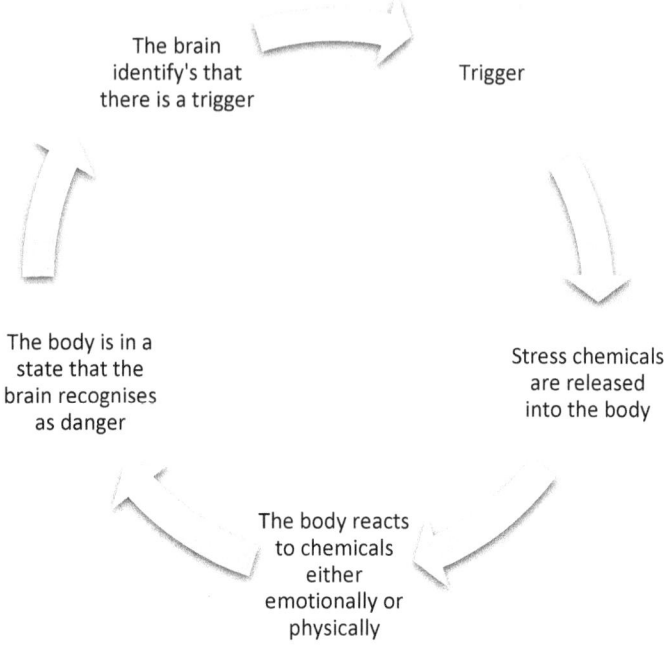

- **Protect** is a state of being where we are in a *Flow of Stress* or a *Cycle of Anxiety*. It is a state of being NOT okay.
- **Pleasure** is a state of being where we are thinking and feeling good. It is a state of being where we ARE okay.
- You have come to this book because you want to learn how to deactivate your state of *Protect*.
- You can't exist in a state of *Protect* and *Pleasure* at the same time.
- Here is the clincher, the ENTIRE POINT of this chapter: **We can deactivate the state of *Protect* by releasing *Pleasure* messaging from our brain into our system.**

- When the cycle of panic and anxiety is in full swing, when the chemicals of *Protect* are being pumped out through your body, the way to move out of that state is to inject *Pleasure* into the cycle.
- Start intentionally injecting pleasure-inducing activities into your days and weeks with a new determination. Self-care in this respect is connected to your emotional and physical health and is an important deactivation tool for your anxiety.
- It's time to take back your life and enjoy it.

chapter 4

gaining altitude with gratitude

As they say in neuroscience, neurons that fire together, wire together. In other words, the more one dwells on negativity, the more and more the brain becomes trapped in negativity and in a self-defeating vicious cycle. What becomes crucial, then, is to create new neural pathways within the brain via new thinking habits to 'interrupt' these ingrained patterns and enable the default mindset to become more positive and calmer.[7]

—Sharee James

It's my hope that in the last chapter, you learnt or were reminded of some things that have unlocked new ways to deactivate anxiety. Knowledge does unlock power in our lives, and it is my aim in the next few chapters to show you how you can interrupt or as I term it 'deactivate' the *Flow of Stress* and the *Cycle of Anxiety*. We will be looking at how to intentionally move from producing *Protect* messages within the *Storehouse of the Mind* and toward producing *Pleasure* ones.

---

7   https://www.ashimaliving.com/how-gratitude-can-reduce-anxiety-and-depression/ 1.10.2020

In the coming chapters, I will offer some practical deactivation tools for the mind, body, and soul. Then we will move into dealing more specifically with the spiritual components that can create anxiety. Finally, I will offer some thoughts on core beliefs and the importance of replacing ungodly root systems in your life—because unhealthy roots produce rotten fruit.

It is the intention of this book to give you simple tools to deactivate your anxiety rather than complex theory. There is place for that, and people for that. It's important—but it is not the heart of this book. So just a warning, don't expect quantum physics, but do anticipate tools to bring practical breakthroughs.

In this chapter then, let's continue looking at practical ways to deactivate your anxiety in mind and body. The tool that I want to share with you at this stage in our journey is a power tool when it comes to 'circuit-breaking' anxiety. It is also very 'on trend' at the moment, and it has revolutionised how I deal with my life. It has been an absolute catalyst for helping me manage and dominate anxiety.

Are you ready for it?

It's gratitude.

It is pretty simple, isn't it? But gratitude is very powerful. Gratitude is quick; it is easy; it is accessible anywhere you are, and most importantly, a genuine state of gratitude is a *Pleasure*-producing activity.

gaining altitude with gratitude

Gratitude will give you a new altitude of perspective over your life. Even if nothing has changed.

I remember when I first experienced gratitude as a deactivator for my anxiety. It was when I had just started intentionally adding *Pleasure* activities into my life, as we discussed in the last chapter.

For me, one of these activities is the God-given experience of having a massage. Can I get an amen, somebody? I knew massages were really enjoyable in theory, but when I lay down on the table, and the massage started, I would often be triggered by the feeling of being trapped on the bed, and so the panic would begin. However, this particular day would turn out to be different.

I remember lying on the massage table and feeling the anxiety rise and take a grip. I then started to follow the process of gratitude that I am going to share with you today. I started to feel the anxiety settling right down, and I could feel the *Protect* chemicals in my body being deactivated, and the *Pleasure* chemicals washing over me. I could literally feel the 'circuit breaker' coming into play, and then all these pleasure chemicals of feeling safe and good, well and creative, started to flow through my body. I couldn't believe it—gratitude worked!

In his book, *What Happy People Know*, Dan Baker states:

> It is a fact of neurology that the brain cannot be in a state of appreciation and a state of fear at the same time. The two states may alternate but are mutually

exclusive.[8]

I must admit, when I first began practicing gratitude and appreciation, it was difficult. The first step in retraining the brain was to not see gratitude for those things in my past or appreciation for those in my present as hard, but just as an **unfamiliar experience.**

It is an interesting note that when you view something new as being difficult, you are actually activating a measure of *Protect*. I have discovered a better way of viewing something new is to reframe it as simply being unfamiliar and as something to call up my curiosity (*Pleasure*), not my apprehension (*Protect*). Hope you are starting to see how this works.

I would sit down with my notepad every day, and it would take all of my might to switch my brain from apprehension into a state of appreciation and begin writing down a 'praise list'. However, I was on a mission because I could see that **I needed to make *Pleasure* a state of familiarity.**

If you find the practice of gratitude unfamiliar, think of it like going to the gym and using muscles that you haven't used for a long time, maybe ever. Initially, it is difficult, unfamiliar, and it doesn't feel right. You've really got to think about what you are doing. Doing this is called conscious incompetence.

Like when you started driving a car. Every brake, every acceleration and pressure on the brake is a conscious

---

8   https://makedapennycooke.com/antidote-to-fear/ 3.10.2020

state of knowing that you don't know what you are doing. However, once you've driven for a while, driving becomes a state of unconscious competence. You have become so familiar with the process that you do it automatically.

It is the same with the practices of gratitude, appreciation, and praise in your brain. When I started, after writing down a list of things I was grateful for I would re-read it over and over again to myself. I would wake up in the morning and re-read what I'd written the night before, and then I'd write down some more.

Initially, you might have to write things down and re-read them to start getting gratitude working. In time though, the new pathways of thinking will move from conscious incompetence to engaging in it so automatically that it becomes engraved in the soul of who you are.

Something that helped me connect with my gratitude when I was really struggling was to think back about my testimony and the grace of Jesus. I just started thinking about where God has turned up in my life, how He looked after me, and how He provided for me.

That's thanksgiving. It is about thinking of the ways that God has come through for you.

I started to think about miracles in my life and miracles in other people's lives. I didn't just think about them; I got *into* that moment. That is a really important part of a 'circuit breaker'. You must get *into* the moment. It's not just about thanking God for my daughter, but it is getting *into* a memory of when she is in my arms, and when I look at her little fingers and little toes and think about her little gummy smile. Even thinking about it now releases pleasure. It is beautiful. She's so beautiful. I'm so thankful, so grateful and full of praise for that.

✏️ **I'd like you to get *into* your moments and** start writing them down. Write down the miracles in your life, testimonies, and things that you are thankful for. Then practise getting into those moments, being in those memories. What were you wearing? What were you feeling? What were you thinking?

As you do that, you will start to produce all those feel-good chemicals and emotions in your body, and your body will love you for it. Your skin loves you for it. Your hair loves you for it. Your heart loves you for it. Your blood pressure loves you for it. Your stomach loves you for it. Your bowels thank you for it.

Your body is so attuned to your stress levels. As I have said before, stress-related issues are a major reason why people go to see their doctors. Your immunity is affected by stress. But when you inject gratitude—when you 'circuit break' your stress with deep gratitude—you get better. It works. The Scriptures have understood the power tool of gratitude long before it became trendy. So, let's shift focus now and take a look at some scriptural advice on this idea of gratitude.

> ... and provide for those who grieve in Zion—to bestow on them a crown of beauty instead of ashes, the oil of joy instead of mourning, and a garment of praise instead of a spirit of despair.
>
> —Isaiah 61:3a

What a stunning verse! This is a beautiful picture of what the presence of God can do in the life of a person. In particular, I want to highlight where we read about God inviting His people to replace a garment of despair with a garment of praise. Despair is a sense of heaviness, oppression, weight, worry, anxiety or depression. God never wanted to leave His people in that state, and so we are given a way out.

We are instructed to replace this heaviness with a garment of praise. A garment of worship, honour, exaltation, adoration, *thankfulness,* and blessing. To be deeply grateful regardless of current circumstances. The important part of this is that **you** need to replace it. **You** need to make the choice in the midst of the anxiety, and in the midst of the worry and stress, to start being grateful. It is a choice, and it is an offering of faith and trust to God.

We may have to make the choice to get our grateful on, but we don't have to do it alone. As I shared with you early on, you are surrendering this whole area to God and asking Him to come and help. Let me give you some practical steps to taking off a garment of despair (anxiety) and putting on a garment of praise (gratitude).

Let's look at Philippians 4:6–7:

> Do not be anxious about anything, but in every situation, by prayer and petition, with thanksgiving, present your requests to God. And the peace of God, which transcends all understanding, will guard your hearts and your minds in Christ Jesus.

The first point is that we don't need to be anxious about anything. I used to think that the activity of worry was my responsibility. That I was being responsible; that I was looking after myself and taking proper control of my life by worrying and being anxious. Once this Scripture really sunk in, I realised that what God was actually saying to me was that I don't need to be anxious. He is giving me permission as His child to do away with that kind of 'self-care'. What freedom we have in Jesus!

Let me take the example of God being our Provider. I remember one day, as I looked at my daughters, it occurred to me that if they started worrying about things like bills and how they would pay for food, that they would be actually showing a distrust in my ability to provide. Of course, they need to show wisdom and faithfulness in what I have given them, but being anxious about it wouldn't show me they believed I was a mum that could look after them, would it?

Likewise, with us and God, the best way for us to

respond to His favour, provision, and love is not to worry, be fearful or get anxious. The best way we can respond to who God is, is to simply offer gratitude, be obedient, and live life fully and on-purpose (amongst other things, all of which are in no way connected to living a life in fear).

Gratitude is our way of showing God that we trust Him.

Philippians doesn't allow us to abdicate our responsibilities in our anxiety, though. So, what are we to do? It directs us to be prayerful and bring our petitions to God. Rather than turning to worry when something comes up, now what we are to do is become prayerful. Let anxiety now be a trigger that bounces you like a springboard to prayer.

Worry and anxiety are still triggers, but they do not begin the *Flow of Stress* or ignite the *Cycle of Anxiety*. Instead, they direct us toward prayer and petition and thanksgiving to God.

Make gratitude a verb

We need to be active in bringing our petitions to God. Write them down if that helps you. Get them out, get them off your shoulders, and give them to God. Replacing the garment of heaviness means bringing your troubles to Jesus and letting Him take on the burden. It is a new way of 'doing' hardship and anxiety, and it is the way we were reborn to follow. When we do this, we engage in the great exchange of the Bible.

In the early days when I needed some help, I would imagine that I could put all the issues I was facing in a box, and I could just hand it over to the Lord and imagine the Lord taking it from me and being completely free of it.

When I was really struggling, and even today, I set up communion in my room, put on some worship music, and allow the symbolism of the communion to be the reality of Jesus in my room.

I'll offload it all, all my pain or sorrow and empty myself of my worries. The key to this is that it is done in faith, in an attitude of gratitude. I don't offload in the absence of worship; I do it in an attitude of worship and thanksgiving.

To honour God in the pain, in the anxiety, is true devotion. Then, I take communion in faith that Jesus has both listened to my heart and troubles and is now replacing the anxiety with His peace. As I take the bread and the juice, I'm in faith receiving Jesus into my body and my anxiety.

This is the great exchange, it is the Cross at work in our lives, the Good News of the Gospel.

The key part comes next, and over the years, I've found that it is the part of the process many people forget.

gaining altitude with gratitude

We need to learn to receive from heaven and to listen for the whispers of the Holy Spirit. To receive in prayer has been more powerful in my life than anything I have ever had to say. In following this process, you are in effect taking off the garment of anxiety by giving your worries to God, and then putting on the garment of praise by receiving His peace and presence in your life.

In this exchange, we allow the work of the Cross to lift our perspective to a higher altitude over our circumstance.

Let us do that right now. Imagine your issue. Is it relational? Is it financial? Is it a fear about the future? Is it a heaviness about the past? What's top of your mind right now? Get it in your mind and heart and let's pray. *Note: Give God some space to move in this prayer, don't rush it.*

🙌 **"Lord, help me to hand it over, trusting that** you care for me, trusting that you will take it. I am grateful in the midst of my anxiety for [fill in what you are grateful for] and here is what I am anxious about [now tell Him all about it].

I believe you want to give me peace; that you will guard my heart and my mind; and that you want to clothe me with thanksgiving and a garment of praise. I open my heart and mind right now to receive your peace. Where I've chosen to be filled with anxiety, I choose now to be filled with your peace and your presence. Amen."

Just let that peace come. Rest in it for a while and wait for Him. Listen to what He has to say.

HIGHLIGHTS

- In this chapter, we looked at practical ways to deactivate your anxiety in both mind and body. The tool I want to share with you in this chapter is the power tool of gratitude.

- Gratitude is quick; it is easy; it is accessible wherever you are, and most importantly, gratitude is a *Pleasure*-producing activity.

- The Scriptures have understood the power tool of gratitude long before it became trendy. We took a look at some scriptural advice.

- In Isaiah 61:3, we read about the idea of God's people replacing a garment of heaviness with a garment of praise. The important part of this is that **you** need to replace yours—but you don't have to do it alone.

- You have permission from God to NOT worry, be anxious or live in fear.

- Gratitude is our way of showing God that we trust Him.

- Make gratitude a verb.

- Handing over our anxieties, and then receiving His peace, is the Great Exchange. It is the Cross at work in our lives, the Good News of the Gospel.

- We need to learn to receive from heaven and to listen for the whispers of the Holy Spirit. Learning to receive in prayer has been more powerful in my life than anything I have ever had to say.

chapter 5

meaningful mindfulness

In the previous chapter, we looked at how gratitude gives us an ability to get altitude over our anxiety. In this chapter, I want to give you another tool that will help you deactivate your anxiety, and which is also an on-trend idea currently circulating. It is a practice that you've probably heard of, and it has helped turn my anxiety around.

It is the practice of mindfulness.

We live in an ever-increasingly fast-paced world. I previously lived in Sydney Australia for 20 years, but I spent my school life in a country town in rural New South Wales. I grew up surrounded by wide open space, trees, mountains, and the bush. This was a huge contrast to Sydney, which is the biggest city in Australia.

The pace of life in Sydney was intense. There certainly weren't many wide-open spaces, and the bush was an hour's drive away. The city seemed to have this buzz to it—like a constant hum of activity. For a country girl, this perpetual buzz had an element of excitement, but it could also drain my soul. I would often retreat to national parks and the ocean for solace and sanity.

I don't think though, that you need to live in Sydney to feel that way. All you need to be is alive and dealing with the pressures of work or school, family, and peers to experience life's pressure. A pressure that, if unmonitored, compresses your inner world and leaves your body in constant stress.

Many of us are going from one thing to the next, taking the kids here, going to work or university, coming home, cooking, doing ministry or being involved in church. Perhaps you are in what feels like Groundhog Day, keeping the house clean, caring for young children and managing your daily routines. Maybe it's dealing with relational issues and pressures or feeling concerned about life and all its complexities.

Let's face it, being an adult or a kid has many stressors or triggers. This is why we need to be intentional and get serious about injecting anxiety deactivators into our lives and teach our kids to do the same. We want to be habitually meeting our stress-filled lives with the production of *Pleasure* messaging.

The quality and the quantity of our lives and our kids' lives are dependent on it.

Mindfulness has been around for a very long time and, of late, is piquing more interest through serious studies. For example, researchers from John Hopkins University in Baltimore looked through 19,000 mediation studies and found there is strong evidence that mediation and mindfulness are beneficial. Some of these benefits included the "ease of psychological stresses like anxiety, depression and pain".[9]

Dr Elizabeth Hoge, a psychiatrist at the Centre for Anxiety and Traumatic Stress Disorders at Massachusetts General Hospital and an assistant professor of psychiatry at Harvard Medical School, believes that people who suffer with anxiety often can't distinguish between a "problem-solving thought and a nagging anxious thought that has no benefit".[10]

"Mindfulness teaches you to recognize, 'Oh, there's that thought again. I've been here before. But it's just that—a thought—and not a part of my core self'," says Dr Hoge.[11]

Now, let me address the idea held by some Christians that mindfulness is a 'New Age' demonic activity. The mindfulness and mediation I am **not** talking about is opening your mind to foreign ideas or entities that are

---
9 https://www.health.harvard.edu/blog/mindfulness-meditation-may-ease-anxiety-mental-stress-201401086967 6.7.2021
10 Ibid.
11 https://www.health.harvard.edu/blog/mindfulness-meditation-may-ease-anxiety-mental-stress-201401086967 6.7.2021

opposed to Jesus. That is called witchcraft, and it isn't the practice I am about to share. The mindfulness that I am talking about is learning to be present, completely present. Present in your body and present to your breath. Present to your surroundings and 100% fully present to God.

Unless we learn to be fully present, we are actually going to miss the Holy Spirit speaking to us. The Holy Spirit speaks to us in our NOW and in our present. Being mindful is a very important discipline, not only to circuit-break your stress, but also as a way of being available to hearing the voice of God.

As you practise this more, you are going to start to hear Him speaking more. I know I certainly did. You are also going to learn to enjoy life far more because you are retraining your brain from a pattern of living in the past or the future and into being absorbed and fully alive in your present. It is a powerful tool.

Since having kids, I have had to learn to be 'with them' and not allow my brain to live in tomorrow or think about what happened yesterday. The practise of mindfulness has helped me to be present with my kids, my husband, and the people I am ministering to. Being mindful is simply being fully present in the here and now.

✏ **So many thoughts that are associated with** anxiety are related to thoughts that are projected and swept up in the 'what-ifs'. Why not grab your journal and have a think about your thought processes when you are stressed? Those thoughts are often at their core ideas around: 'what if this had happened?' or 'what if this will happen?'

When you learn to become present in your body, and aware of your surroundings and God being with you, you actually deactivate the part of the brain that stimulates your 'fight or flight' response. Perhaps think of the last time you experienced anxiety. Perhaps it's now? Write down what goes through your mind and look at these thoughts objectively. Are they around the ideas of 'what if?' or of the past or future? If so, mindfulness will be a gift to you.

I learnt this for myself when I was having a very bad episode of panic in the period that I have shared about previously, just after my eldest daughter was born. At the time, I also had been put on an anti-depressant/anxiety medication, which unknown to us at the time, was giving me a psychotic side effect. I felt like the adrenalin and all those *Protect* chemicals that were pumping from my brain into my body were actually acid, burning me alive from the inside. While my psychologist was reworking the medication, she also gave me some mindfulness work to try, and so I put headphones on, and I stayed awake all night long with this mindfulness meditation playing on repeat. Although the reaction was still happening, the heightened panic lessened significantly, and I discovered mindfulness worked!

I would like to share with you an exercise that has not only worked for me, but also countless clients that I have worked with over the years. It is retraining your brain from the 'what-ifs' into a place of being centred and disciplined in thought. Below I am going to give you a mindfulness exercise that is basic, and then at the end of this chapter, I have given you links to two more *De Activating Anxiety* Christian Mindfulness Meditations. These are guided exercises that I have done for you that can be watched and listened to on YouTube.

Mindfulness exercise 1

Take three big deep breaths. Slow your mind and breathe in and out three times.

Bring to Jesus whatever is top of mind or heavy of heart. Trust that He can carry it for the next few minutes, while you fully centre your thoughts and attention on this exercise. Hand the worries over.

Take another long slow breath in and release it out.

This time, as you breathe, I want you to listen to your breath as it goes in and then feel the breath as it goes out. We are going to do three more breaths. Listen and feel the breath. Bring your mind back as we do this. If your mind starts to wander, don't be angry, just bring your mind back and listen to the breath.

Take your time.

This time, as you breathe, I want you to feel your feet on the floor. Are they in shoes? Or are you barefoot? What does it feel like? Feel your feet; be in your feet. Think of your feet. Breathe in and out three times as you think about how your feet feel.

Now, feel your legs as you breathe. Are you sitting? Can you feel pants on your skin? Where is your bottom? Can you feel the pressure of your bottom on the seat? What about your back? Keep breathing in and out—nice and slowly.

Take your time.

Become aware of your shoulders, your arms. Just be really aware of your body. Be in your body. Be present in your body. If your brain starts to think about things, just gently bring it back to your body. Breathe in and become really aware of your breath as you breathe out.

Now, just breathe in and out at your own pace. Become really aware of your body and of your surroundings. What is in the room?

This time, as you breathe in, I want you to look at something in the room and become really aware of it. Look at the shape, the colour. Still breathing, become really aware, really conscious, really focussed on what that is. Breathing in and breathing out. Study that item and be curious about it as you look at it.

Take three slow breaths, in and out.

Take your mind to something else in the room, and breathe in and out. Become really aware of it. Is it a photo frame? Is it a fan? What is it? Look at the corners. Look at the centre. Just be in the moment, looking and investigating and being curious. Breathing in and breathing out.

Now, close your eyes and take three slow deep breaths, in and out, and just sit in the moment. Be aware of your body and study it. And, when you are ready, open your eyes and come back to the book.

End.

Really simple, right? How did you go with it? Was it hard to keep your mind centred on the breaths? Was it hard to keep your mind from wandering? If it was, all it is telling you is that this is an amazing area that you can start practising.

Mindfulness is being aware and learning to be in the now. It is so important and such a wonderful power tool to circuit-break stress and the anxiety.

As you go forward into this day, I'd love you to practise this tool. The idea is to breathe slowly and become aware of your body and your breath. This centres your thoughts into your present. While breathing slowly and mindfully, choose items in your view to study.

Training your brain is possible, and it is key to deactivating the *Protect* train of thought you have built up over the years.

I have also done two other 'live' guided mindfulness meditations for you. These use Scripture as the basis for the meditation, whilst also concentrating on the body and the breath. You can find them at:

https://larissademichiel.com/resource

Give them a try, and I'd love to know in the comments of the videos how you go.

Remember, it's my desire that this book is not just an information delivery, but also an encounter between you and the Holy Spirit. I want you to read through the chapters, engage with the activities, and pray the prayers—all the while experiencing the transformation that can only come from Jesus and His victory on the Cross. So, as you do these mediations, let's be expectant that the Holy Spirit is with you.

HIGHLIGHTS

- Being an adult or a kid has many stressors or triggers, which is why we need to be intentional about injecting anxiety deactivators into our lives.

- Mindfulness is a great way to do just that.

- The Holy Spirit speaks to us in our NOW and in our present. Being mindful is a very important practice—not only to circuit-break your stress, but also as a way of being available to hearing the voice of God.

- Practise the tools of mindfulness I have given you and be sure to be aware that the Holy Spirit is there in your experience with you.

- You can participate now in some mindful exercises I have done for you.
Head to https://larissademichiel.com/resource

chapter 6

activating tender loving care

It is my firm belief and has been my prayer, that as you read the pages of this book, deep transformation will take place within you. That, as you engage in the activities and pray the prayers, not only will you find breakthrough and healing for your mind, but **you will experience it in your body also.**

Many of you who are reading this book are dealing with ailments, aches, and disease as a result of unresolved anxiety. I am convinced that Jesus wants to use this book to be the truth you have been waiting for—the truth that will set you free and supernaturally heal you. If this sounds like you; if you are experiencing disease in your body and sense there is a link to your stress and anxiety, then I invite you to place your hand on your heart and pray this prayer in faith over your life?

👏 **"Father, I come to you with this disease** [name it]. Lord, I pray for supernatural healing in Jesus' name. I believe that, as I am being transformed and renewed in my mind, you can also transform and heal my body as well. I pray Romans 8:11(NLT) into my body:

> The Spirit of God, who raised Jesus from the dead, lives in [me]. And just as God raised Christ Jesus from the dead, He will give life to [my] mortal [body] by this same Spirit living within [me].

I thank you Lord, that the fruit of this prayer will be a healthy body and mind. In Jesus' name, Amen."

> Don't you realise that your body is the temple of the Holy Spirit, who lives in you and was given to you by God?
>
> —1 Corinthians 6:19a (NLT)

Ok, I'd like to just cut to the chase with you in the beginning of this chapter. Looking after yourself, your mind, your body, and your soul is in fact a godly practise. Sure, it can become out of order and become a form of idolatry, but what I am talking about is caring for yourself out of the revelation that your body houses God and is His vehicle on the earth.

I see many Christians (and this was my story too) who are passionate about their spiritual lives but forgo giving attention to their earthly bodies. They are disciplined about reading the Word of God (which is brilliant) but are not as

activating tender loving care

disciplined about looking after their health.

> And what do you benefit if you gain the whole world but lose your own soul?
>
> —Matthew 16:26 (NLT)

Is there anything worth losing your own soul over? When I was on the road to recovery after my breakdown in my mid-thirties, I remember reading Matthew 16:26 and being hit with the Scripture in a new way. I had always read it as losing your soul eternally, but on this day, I saw it in a new light and felt the Holy Spirit whisper something fresh. I felt Him say, "Larissa, what good is it for you to minister and work hard to witness to the whole world, if you lose your own soul's health in the process? Is anything more important than the state of your soul? Larissa, you matter to me—all of you."

If I am brutally honest, I was completely burnt out. I was tired, frustrated and bored in ministry. I had been running on the fumes of passion for God, but in running hard, I had neglected the care of my body and soul. It was in this moment, however, as I read this Scripture that I felt the tender voice of God telling me that I mattered more than my purpose. That I would fizzle out before I had completed my mission on the planet if I didn't start to bring some love and care to this temple. I needed to prioritise me in the equation if I was to truly live life to the fullest.

Many of you reading this book can identify with this.

You are passionate about fulfilling your life's purpose and growing as a person in Christ, but you opened the pages of this book because your internal world is struggling. Amazing child of God, here is a bite of wisdom for you: you may just be in need of some tender loving care (TLC). That will only happen though if you give yourself permission for it to happen. If you become intentional about making the necessary changes.

As I said earlier in this book, the relationship between anxiety and disease is irrefutable. If we are going to run our race to the finish line in this life, and do so in optimum health internally and externally, then we must take care of the bodies God has entrusted to us. We must see that task in fact as imperative to our overall success.

I heard a story once about how a great athlete, a sprinter, was asked, "What is one of the most important things you do for your race?" He said, "I check my shoelaces are tied correctly." And I thought, "How true!" Years of preparation and training can be demolished if the simplest discipline of tying your shoelaces properly is overlooked.

Sometimes it's the little things that if unattended become the reason you trip up in your race.

It wouldn't have mattered how strict his training had been or how passionate he was. If he had tripped on undone shoelaces, his race was going to be affected. I am

activating tender loving care

convinced that a lot of the anxiety, stress, and fear we may be feeling today is, in part, due to some simple things that we could be doing that we're not.

Addressing our self-talk, having quiet times with God, injecting *Pleasure* activities from your list in chapter 3 and being connected to community are all examples of life-giving, TLC gifts we can give ourselves. If we are going to change our lives, we need to insert these habits of self-care into our lives. In this chapter, I want to discuss some other simple changes we can make that will provide much needed TLC.

The first simple TLC activity I'd love you to think about is exercise. Exercise is so important for our mental health and wellbeing. Let's think back to the premise of this book. We are looking at ways to deactivate *Protect* messaging that is coming from our minds and into our bodies. That messaging causes chemicals to be released into our bodies. What happens to these substances? Well, as we have learnt, if we don't deal with the stress, these chemicals become a form of disease.

Think back to the *Flow of Stress* for a moment. If you can trap your thoughts and take your thoughts captive at the trigger stage of the *Flow of Stress*, then you can stop a lot of those *Protect* chemicals from pumping into your system. This is why changing your perceptions of your triggers is so important. However, if you don't cut the anxiety off at the trigger stage, then stress chemicals are released into your body, and you need to manage a *Cycle of Anxiety*. A powerful way you can deal with the release of those chemicals in your body is to exercise them out.

Exercise not only deals with *Protect* chemicals that are released in your body, but also increases your *Pleasure* chemicals from the *Storehouse of the Mind*. Exercise is your natural way of getting high!

I like to combine my daily exercise with prayer and worship. Combining worship and prayer or a great podcast with my exercise also increases the likelihood of me doing it. You combine these things with sunlight, and you are giving your body a huge gift. Sunlight is nature's way of giving you a warm hug—make sure you are getting it!

Another practical tip is eating healthy natural unprocessed food as often as we can. There are many opinions on how and what we should eat, and I am in no way an expert. I have some thoughts though. I think it's pretty obvious that what we put into our bodies is going to make a difference to what we are getting out of them. If we are putting junk in regularly, we are going to feel like junk. As the old saying goes, 'you are what you eat'.

Although serotonin is well known as a brain neurotransmitter, it is estimated that 90% of the body's serotonin is made in the digestive tract.[12]

---

12   https://www.caltech.edu/about/news/microbes-help-produce-serotonin-gut-46495 19.06.2019

activating tender loving care

✏️ **How we feel can be related to the food we** put in our bodies. You just have to watch either of my children after red cordial to see the effect of what we eat can have on our mood. Why not track it? For a week, just as an experiment, take a diary of what you eat and your moods. You might discover some interesting information about your moods and your food intake.

It might also be worth tracking when you eat. You may find that eating at high stress times for instance can have a bad effect on your digestion and mood too. So, be mindful of how and what you are fuelling your body with.

Another very practical way of deactivating anxiety in your body is, of course, drinking water. If these chemicals have been released in your body, then we want to flush these toxins out where possible. My mum always said, "More exercise, Larissa, and more water will cure all." I would say she has overexaggerated its power (let's not tell her I said that), but there is a lot of truth to it nonetheless.

Here is a great idea: Why not go for a walk, in the sun, listening to worship, and drink water on your return? Right- there is a free, easy, and doable infusion of deactivators that you can do anywhere. To add to it, when you get ready for bed, why not go over your list (that you created in Chapter 3) of *Pleasure* inducing activities and make a plan for this weekend? Or get out your gratitude list and mull over it?

And now you are really getting intentional!

The idea of these deactivators is that you work them into your daily habits. Not huge shifts, but small inserts into your life that will make a world of difference. Another area to think about is talking to your GP. Have you had your iron checked lately? Or your Vitamin D or B levels? It's really important that you include your GP in this journey. Let them know about what has been going on for you in relation to anxiety and request a full check-up. I'm all for having holistic care and know that sometimes anxiety in the body is related to deficiencies that maybe only a doctor can find.

While you are there, I would urge you to ask them about further expert help. Talk to them about your symptoms and what there is on offer to support you. Seeing a counsellor or psychologist may very well be your next best step. The amount of healing I found when I talked to a trained psychologist was black and white. You may also want to talk to your GP about medication.

I know there is a stigma around this, especially in Christian circles. There is still a culture of shame in many churches around mental health, and this is the reason why I'd like to spend the rest of the chapter discussing medication for depression and anxiety. I certainly carried my own baggage because of this when it came to medication related to mental health.

I was a drug addict when I first came to the Lord. As a result of where I had been rescued from, I had a deep conviction that I was never going to touch drugs again. I mean any drugs! I didn't take Panadol, and I didn't drink coffee. I was a puritan when it came to any form of drugs, but in truth, this was born out of a deep fear of ever going back to the life I was saved out of.

A few years into being a Christian, I felt the call to do a missionary stint in the Northern Territory of Australia. I was going to be out there for 3–6 months, and my mum wanted me to go and get up to date with my vaccinations. I really wrestled with God over it because I thought, "Is that a drug? Is it not a drug?" I decided that maybe there was wisdom in having them updated, and I went and saw the doctor. I followed the peace of God in my decision.

When I saw the doctor, she said to me that I needed to have some check-ups, and I thought, "Oh well, that's fine." It came back that there was an abnormality and that I needed to go and be checked out further. After the second check-up, it came back that I did in fact have Stage II cancer.

I battled with the news because I thought, "God, you can heal me! I won't take the drugs needed for the surgery, and I don't need doctors when I have a miracle working God. I know Jesus can miraculously heal me. He miraculously healed me from drugs. He miraculously healed me from a large lump in my throat, and He can miraculously heal me in this too."

I had decided no surgery, no doctors, and no medication, and then God spoke.

In the midst of my indignation about this surgery, I sensed the Holy Spirit speak to me one very simple sentence that changed everything. He said, "Larissa, I AM your healer, and I WILL heal you in MY WAY."

It was like instantaneously I knew that God would heal me in the way He decided. That being healed is the miracle, whether in a moment or as part of a process using doctors.

The point was that I was to be led by the Holy Spirit in how God wanted to heal me, not in my religious indoctrination. In this case, the miracle would come through the doctor's hands. I was convicted, and I was set upon his path to be healed.

Getting in to have the operation in itself was full of the miraculous and was an opportunity to witness to a number of doctors. I learnt a big lesson that has set me up for the rest of my life. I learnt to always be guided by the Holy Spirit in my healing, rather than dictating to God how my healing should happen.

What was true in that season became true in my season of debilitating mental health. He led me to receive healing, in part, through the avenue of medication. I am not going to tell you though that in the early days I didn't wrestle with it, because I did!

"I was a pastor," I thought. "Shouldn't I be faith-filled enough to have control over my own mind? I mean, what sort of Pentecostal, born again, Spirit-filled Christian was I to need medical intervention?"

activating tender loving care

I now know the answer to these questions! I am a child of God who is committed to following God's healing for my life, wherever He chooses to lead me. And so are you.

When I had cancer, I went and sought treatment. No one I know would tell me that by doing so I was somehow lacking faith or removing myself from God's healing. In taking the medication that was offered to me, I was not giving up my trust in God, I was believing for healing in the process.

I had a strong chemical imbalance in my mind, and I needed medication to help me get into a place where I could use the tools that I am sharing with you.

I've heard it said that medication is like a ladder being offered to you out of a large dark hole you're trapped in. It helps you find your way out while still requiring you to use the steps. For some, without medication (the ladder) there is no way of taking the first step toward their healing! In order for me to have been able to use the tools and strategies that I'm sharing with you in these pages, I needed medical support. You might too.

I decided a long time ago, after a long wrestle with all this, that I wouldn't be shamed for using medication. And neither should you if you need it. Medication is not the answer for many, but sometimes the panic, stress, and the anxiety are so severe, and life is so overwhelming, that taking medication is the right course of action. If you think that might be you, then the next best step in your healing is to talk to your GP and be open to God's healing through medical intervention.

I want to encourage you not to battle with the stigma of mental illness, medication or an ill-informed Christian worldview. Be led by the Holy Spirit on how you are going to find your healing. If that means going to a health practitioner and taking some medication—it may be for a short period of time or it may be for life—do follow peace.

If you had diabetes, you might be on medication for life. If you had liver problems, you might be on medication for life. If you had HIV/AIDS, you might be on medication for life. But it wouldn't make you any less faithful. Don't be swept up in silly 'Christianese' that puts God in a box with how He should heal you.

This chapter has been about encouraging you to look after yourself by including simple habits into your days. Let me end by encouraging you with this. I was flying with my daughter this week, and as per usual, I was given instructions from the flight attendant. She told me that, in case of emergency, I needed to put on my own oxygen mask before helping my daughter with hers. This is not because the flight attendant is heartless, nor would I be a monstrous mother if I do so. By making the decision to apply my oxygen mask first, I am better equipped to look after my daughter. By making sure I am full of oxygen, and full of health in my mind, body, and soul, I am actually setting myself up to be able to love my family and friends at my best and for my longest.

"Father, thank you that we are on a journey. We know not everything is going to be fixed and tied up in a beautiful bow over this time together, but we do want to get out of this book everything that You would want us for us. Father, show me any practical ways that I might be contributing to my anxiety, and help me make the changes necessary so that I can be internally well and run my race.
In Jesus' name, Amen."

HIGHLIGHTS

- Don't you realise that your body is the temple of the Holy Spirit, who lives in you and was given to you by God? 1 Corinthians 6:19a.

- I'd like to just cut to the chase with you: looking after yourself, your mind, your body, and your soul is in fact a godly practise. Here are simple ways to practically deactivate anxiety in your day-to-day life.

    1. Exercise
    2. Eating well
    3. Checking all your blood work for deficiency
    4. Drinking more water
    5. Visiting your GP

- Be open to how God wants to heal you and be led by His Spirit.

- By making sure I am full of oxygen, and full of health in my mind, body, and soul, I am actually setting myself up to be able to love my family, friends, and my world of influence at my best and for my longest.

chapter 7

let's get spiritual

Well done, we have arrived at the halfway mark along this journey together. Up until this point I have wanted to focus on the practical ways of managing and deactivating your anxiety when it comes to your mind and body.

Pleasure inducing activities, getting a good understanding of what happens in your physical body, upping your gratitude and mindfulness, making small healthy changes in your routine, and seeing your GP are all powerful and simple strategies to manage your anxiety.

Now I would like to set off for the next leg of our adventure together by focussing on what makes us distinctive as Christians, and that is activating our spirituality.

Having our spirits made alive in Christ, and subsequently being able to receive from the Holy Spirit, into our human spirit is an imperative anxiety deactivator for our earthly bodies.

I am convinced that it is our birthright as sons and daughters of our heavenly Father to be able to hear from

Him. It is not just something that we desperately need in life, but it is something that God is passionate about. Do you trust that He wants to be heard?

From the beginning of time through to Revelation, God shows us it is His desire that we should hear from Him.

Remember, in the Garden of Eden God walked with Adam and Eve and spoke to them? In the Old Testament, God spoke to His people through the patriarchs. He spoke to the people of God through Moses, Aaron, and Miriam. He spoke through the prophets and the writers of the Old Testament. God's intention was that His people would hear Him.

God the Father then sends Jesus as the WORD OF GOD—are you getting the idea? Jesus' entire life is the voice of God expressing itself on the earth. Jesus' life is the sound of God for all who will listen. Are you wanting to know what God's voice sounds like? Then read the life of Jesus, His words, and His death on the Cross, and you will get a sense of what His voice sounds like.

Then on the day of Pentecost, what do we read happens as the Holy Spirit is poured out in the upper room? As the disciples are obediently waiting for what Jesus had promised after His ascension, we read what looked like "tongues of fire" came upon each person. This tells me that God's intention was to continue to be heard under the New

Covenant, which is a promise for you and me.

> My sheep listen to my voice; I know them, and they follow me.
>
> —John 10:27

If only it was that easy to hear God in the midst of all the noise of life, right? I don't know about you, but over the years, I have wrestled with what's God's voice and what's the devil's. In order to help those of you asking the same questions, this chapter is written for you. I'd like to start by discussing what is foreign to God—which is the voice of the devil.

Firstly, I don't agree that having a belief in the reality of Satan belongs in the Dark Ages. In fact, if we are going to embrace the whole victory Jesus has won for us in this life, then we need to have a Biblical worldview on Satan. Jesus spent huge parts of His ministry dealing with demonic forces, and I would encourage you to read over the Gospels again if you are unsure.

As we think about the influence of the demonic and our worldview, we need to make sure it is a Biblical one, not one shaped by our culture of apathy or one of unhealthy obsession. I feel many Christians can fall into one of two camps when it comes to the demonic. Some believe the devil is under every stone and give him credit for every activity under the sun. But others are of the opinion that the devil is not real or at least is of no consequence in their lives. I would like to offer that there is another alternative on how the devil affects the Christian life, one that relies on Scripture to shape our views.

The devil is described in many ways in the Scriptures, including Accuser of Christians, Satan, Destroyer, Prince of the Air, The Evil One, Antichrist, Lawless One, Enemy, Prince of Lies, and the One that comes to steal, kill, and destroy. His end goal is the destruction of God's people because he knows that his time is finite.

He's intent on causing as much suffering as he can to humanity with the time he has left. Here is my favourite piece of information though, and a truth that we must hold in the core of our spiritual worldview: The devil was defeated by Jesus at Calvary. He and his demons have all been overcome by the death of Jesus on the Cross and are destined for Hell.

It's not a great ending for them, but a fantastic situation for us. For although demons are not thrown in the everlasting fire yet, they have been conquered, and their ultimate end is coming and certain. Therefore, as Christians it is our responsibility to understand our authority in Christ.

> And having disarmed the powers and authorities, he [Jesus] made a public spectacle of them, triumphing over them by the cross.
>
> —Colossians 2:15

Public spectacle and public humiliation, these are ways we must be thinking about our engagement with the devil. Not as some unrestrained threat to us, but as an entity that is under the feet of Jesus. The kicker is, if we have accepted Jesus as Lord and Saviour, Jesus lives within us. We will discuss our authority more in a future chapter, but for now it is important I make this point:

The devil is subject to Jesus, and Jesus has given us delegated authority on the earth.

Jesus has most certainly given us authority and power to no longer be under the influence of the devil. This includes not having to listen to his counsel. I can hear you asking, "Larissa, what does he 'sound like' then? How do I know if I am listening to him?"

Great question, here are some examples of what the devil's dialect sounds like.

Accusation: He will come at you with accusations of what you have or haven't done. Revelation 12:10 tells us he is in fact "the Accuser of the brethren". So don't feel bad if you have allowed him to attack you because he is a professional (just ask Job). But know that if it sounds accusatory, it is not how God speaks.

Condemnation: Jesus said it best, "Neither do I condemn you; go and sin no more" John 8:11. Jesus didn't come into the world with words or a spirit of condemnation. He came to invite and woo the world to come to Him. Nothing about Jesus' life says He wants to weigh us down with our burdens or sins. Yes, He will convict us, but condemnation and conviction are two different experiences. We must learn the difference.

Confusion: "For God is not *the author* of confusion, but of peace, as in all churches of the saints" 1 Corinthians 14:33. Do you get completely muddled sometimes about the way forward? Lots of thoughts and anxiety about how we will pull this off or that? That is not the way our Creator leads us.

Death: "The enemy has come to kill, steal and destroy" John 10:10. Ideas and thoughts that want to destroy the plan of God, kill the promises of God, and destroy Kingdom Come are straight from the Evil One. So many of my panic attacks were anchored in fear of death.

The devil is a liar, and therefore you can be assured that whatever he says is neither the heart of God for you nor the truth.

The devil would love nothing more than getting our attention. However, I have come to learn, the best way to recognise the devil is to focus on Jesus. To keep Jesus at the front and centre of our lives is the ultimate strategy for recognising foreign ideas. By keeping our focus on God, reading His word, being around people that know Him, and having worship music playing throughout the day, we are becoming familiar with what God sounds like. As we mediate on His promises, allow gratitude and appreciation to guide our thoughts, and learn to be mindful of Him through the day, we become intimate with what His presence feels like.

We recognise a person's voice because of consistent exposure.

If you desire to become more confident in the voice of God, then make spending time with Him your greatest pleasure! We don't have to learn all about the devil's voice by spending time with him. If I turned off all the lights at night-time in a church and then asked you to follow the sound of my voice, you wouldn't need to investigate the dark corners to obey the command. You would simply walk toward the sound of my voice.

The best way to know the devil's voice is to concentrate on God's.

Many of us are listening and entertaining anxiety, worry, fear, confusion, and thoughts of accusation. We are sitting down and having a cuppa with the spirit of condemnation, but Jesus is calling us away from the dark corner.

God is giving us permission to simply disconnect from that voice and turn to Him. God's voice is like the warmest and safest hug you have ever had. His voice empowers you to walk up the steepest mountains and down the deepest valleys. His voice sounds like pure wisdom and clarity. It is so familiar, as though it has been a voice speaking to you since you have been in your mother's womb.

His voice beckoned you when you were a sinner with love and grace. His voice fills your heart, soul, and mind with the understanding that you are known deeply. God's voice sounds like your best day, feels like your most precious memory, and sounds like your most trusted friend's counsel.

I don't often hear God like I might hear my husband speaking, although I have at times had this experience. Mostly, I hear God speaking when I read my Bible or in prayer. It is what I call a sense, a feeling or a thought that lines up Scripture and the Spirit of Christ.

To know the voice of God is to know the presence of God.

The only time I ever heard the audible voice of God was when I was 21, living a complete car crash of a life and hating Christianity. That's when Jesus thought it would be the best time for me to hear an audible voice (the irony doesn't escape me). I heard that voice say, "Jesus Christ is the Son of God." I have never heard that again, but I have heard the small still voice of God from that day till this one.

My point is, if God could be heard by me in that most unholy time of life, how much more can we trust that He wants to be heard by us now? Hearing God's voice, unction, and direction aren't for the really good Christians (there isn't such a thing FYI). They are for all who follow Him. Is that you? If it is, then hearing His voice, as I said at the beginning, is your birthright.

As we move forward, let's make an agreement together that we are going to trust that God wants to hear from us and wants us to hear from Him. There will be lots of opportunity as the chapters come for you to listen to what He might want to say—are you ready?

✎ I'd like you to take out your journal and think through some of these questions.

1. What might stop you from believing that you can hear God?

2. What might God's voice sound like for you?

3. If God has been speaking to you, what has He said over the years? Pop down any time you feel over the years He might have been with you, and what He might have wanted to say.

4. Have you been listening to the devil in any way? If so what aspect of his character from the list below

has been informing your thoughts? What are those thoughts?

- Accuser
- Condemnation
- Confusion
- Death.

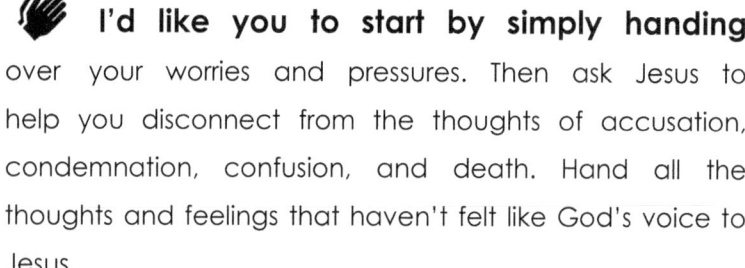 **I'd like you to start by simply handing** over your worries and pressures. Then ask Jesus to help you disconnect from the thoughts of accusation, condemnation, confusion, and death. Hand all the thoughts and feelings that haven't felt like God's voice to Jesus.

Then ask Jesus what He might want to say to you today. The key here is to give yourself and God time. Wait and listen and trust that He will speak. It might be one word, one Scripture or one picture. I always find it helps to have some worship music playing in the background.

Now, write down what Jesus might be saying. The only way to build this area to practice and have a go.

HIGHLIGHTS

- It is our birthright to hear from God.

- From the beginning of time through to Revelation, God shows that it is His desire that His people would hear from Him.

- "My sheep listen to my voice; I know them, and they follow me" John 10:27.

- I don't believe that accepting and acknowledging the reality of Satan belongs in the Dark Ages. In fact, if we are going to embrace the whole victory Jesus has won for us in this life, then we need to have a Biblical worldview of Satan.

- Jesus spent huge parts of His ministry dealing with demonic forces, and I would encourage you to read over the Gospels again if you are unsure.

- So, what does it 'sound like' when we are listening to the accent of the demonic? Accusations, condemnations, confusion, and death are some examples of how the enemy speaks to us.

- We can be assured though that the devil is a liar.

- The best way to know the devil's voice is to concentrate on God's.

- We recognise a person's voice because of consistent exposure.

- God gives us permission to simply disconnect from the devil's voice and turn to Him.

- God's voice is pure and familiar, like a voice you have heard since you were in your mother's womb.

- God's voice sounds like your best day, feels like your most precious memory, and sounds like your most trusted friend's counsel.

- The Cross means He has broken into your life and has something to say. Are you open to hearing Him today?

chapter 8

taking a stand

I think we produce thoughts much like a water pump produces water—one of the handheld types that you might find out on a farm that's connected to a well of water. When you are pumping that water up, you don't pump both clean water and dirty water at the same time. You are either doing one or the other, right? Wherever we draw our water from will determine the quality of that water. This is a great example of how our thought-lives can work, and the spiritual wells that we are drawing from.

When I am working with my clients in a coaching session, I have often asked the question, "Which counsellor are you listening to in this situation? Are you listening to the counsellor of living water or are you listening to the counsellor of stagnant waters?" In this chapter, let's continue looking at the spiritual aspect associated with anxiety.

> Therefore, take up the full armour of God, so that when the day of evil comes, you <u>will be able to stand your ground</u> ...
>
> —Ephesians 6:14(BSB)

For many if not all of us, the devil has been counselling us since we were children. His ideas have shaped our entire worldview. He has shaped our perspectives on parts of our family history, the events in our past, present, and future, and our identities. The world we have grown up in has been infected with the disease of sin, and the reality of these lies has been the plumbline by which we have modelled our lives. This is why the sanctification process is key to our transformation.

We must continually allow the truth of God's word, breathed by His Spirit to set us free.

One of the most potent ideas that the enemy plants for those of us dealing with anxiety is one seeded in fear. Fear is the accent of the enemy, and he wields it, dominates with it, and uses it to oppress all who have come into agreement with his ideas.

I remember during my second nervous breakdown, I had been given medication that turned my levels of anxiety from an 8 to a 20, increasing it to the point where I could hear the intrusive thoughts so loudly in my head and see images so clearly that they were like horror movies on repeat. I felt like there was acid pumping through my body, I came out in welts, and I kept having vivid imaginings of killing myself.

My mum had been living with us on and off by this stage for months, but on this day, she received an emergency phone call that meant she had to return home. My anxieties spun out of control again, and I began throwing up, which in this season was not abnormal, and I nose-dived again into the abyss.

    I tried everything I knew to deal with the levels of anxiety. I went for a walk; I activated my gratitude. I put on my Mindfulness App, but nothing was bringing me back into my rightful mind. I remember lying on the bed in my daughter's room, desperate for peace and a sound mind, when an old song came on from the 80s by Pat Benatar, *Hit Me with Your Best Shot*. Who knew 80s rock would be used by God to speak to me?

    I remember thinking, "That's it! Do your best! Anxiety! Panic! Fear! I am exhausted trying to fight you. Just do it! Bring it on! I'll take it all, I'm done fighting you." And something miraculous happened within about thirty seconds to a minute, I felt deep peace come over me. What had just happened? I needed to work it out because I knew whatever had just happened had deactivated my anxiety in that moment.

What I discovered was that, in accepting the anxiety, I had stopped trying to fight it in my own strength.

    I stopped trying to flee and run from it. I stopped trying to attack it or retreat from it. I had a light bulb moment, if the 'fight or flight' response is what is causing the fear or panic, then choosing not to run from it or fight it was actually choosing not to produce all those chemicals and hormones. By choosing not to engage with the 'fight or flight' messages, but rather choosing to accept it, I was unintentionally disarming the anxiety and circuit-breaking the fear.

Afterwards, I remember thinking, "Can that be good? Can that be godly? Choosing not to fight it or run from it? Choosing to let it slide? Saying, 'Whatever! Do whatever'? Can that really be of God?"

I asked God to help me make sense of this all, because I didn't want to be, for example, surrendering to an ungodly spirit just to gain internal control of my thoughts. The Lord took me on a journey with this—one that I would love to take you on too. It started in Ephesians.

Ephesians 6:13 tells us, "In the day of evil, if you've done all else to stand. Stand therefore." What exactly is this saying? When you've done all that you know to do, when you're trusting in God, when you've got your life right and your heart right, but you are under assault—just stand.

What I could see was that I wasn't surrendering to a spirit of fear at all. I was actually using the power of a surrendered life to give God full control. I was saying, "I actually can't fight this intimidation from an unseen source. So God, I will trust you to fight on my behalf." I then felt the Holy Spirit take me to another Scripture from the Book of Exodus.

At this stage in the story, we find Moses and the

Israelites are still in Egypt and God is about to exercise His power with the last of the ten plagues. This would devastate the Egyptians but secure the freedom of the Israelites after their 400 years of slavery. In Exodus 12:23, Moses instructs the elders to have all the people put the blood of sacrificed spotless lambs around their doorframes. Moses then said,

> When the LORD goes through the land to strike down the Egyptians, he will see the blood on the top and sides of the doorframe and will pass over that doorway, and he will not permit the destroyer to enter your houses and strike you down.

From this Scripture, God was speaking to me about the power of 'standing' because of the victory that was won for me on the Cross. This Scripture speaks to a New Testament Christian from the Old Testament Book of Exodus through to the power of Christ's blood. Those of us who have received Jesus as our Lord and Saviour are reminded every time that we take communion of the victory over our lives, which has already been fought for and won because of Jesus. His blood testifies to all the powers of darkness and fear that they have no power to destroy us.

There are times to fight and times to rebuke, and we will discuss this in more detail in the next few chapters, but before any of that, we must learn to stand in God. We must allow the revelation that it is Jesus who fights for us, in us and through us, and never rely on our own capability.

When we acknowledge that it is the blood of Jesus that is over our lives, protecting us, and in so doing, we instruct the destroyer to pass over us. That is what I was doing that night, when I ceased from fighting or fleeing.

Jesus is asking you to trust Him in this process because you have the blood of Jesus on the doorway of your soul.

Let me make this point very clear, THE DEVIL IS A LIAR, and we must be mindful about the thoughts we allow ourselves to entertain. Are they thoughts that are coming from the wellspring of life, or are they thoughts that are coming from muddy waters that foster death and decay?

> Finally, brothers and sisters, whatever is true, whatever is noble, whatever is right, whatever is pure, whatever is lovely, whatever is admirable—if anything is excellent or praiseworthy—think about such things.
> —Philippians 4:8

When we are slowing our minds down and looking at the thoughts that are coming to us, we need to ask ourselves, is it noble, praiseworthy or excellent? Are these thoughts producing life? And if they are not, then it is likely we are drawing from the wrong body of water.

Corinthians 10:5 says, "We demolish arguments and every pretension that sets itself up against the knowledge of God, and we take captive every thought to make it obedient to Christ." This tells us that we do have a choice in the thoughts we think. We don't have to engage with every thought that comes into our minds.

So why do we? I think it is because we have been trained in fear and anxious thoughts since we were kids. Most of us didn't have Christian parents that taught us how to cast our anxieties on God, therefore we haven't known how to deal with these fearful ideas and feelings.

We haven't been taught to stand and let demonic thoughts pass by.

These thoughts of fear and anxiety are now so familiar to us that we are convinced they are our own. We just feel like our thoughts of destruction are us; our fears are us. Our anxieties are us. But in fact, perhaps, some of our deepest fears are in fact ideas that have been seeded by the enemy. And God is saying to us, "I did not counsel you in these ideas. You can let them go; let them pass by."

I felt that I really needed that permission to disengage from thoughts of anxiety. I had always thought that I needed to analyse these thoughts of impending doom. That to be in control and safe, I had to investigate all the 'what-ifs' that would spring up in my thought life. I thought it was my responsibility to have answers to these anxieties and engage in them in order to be okay. What a lie from those muddy waters.

God says that if they are not true, if they are not praiseworthy, if they are not correct, you have permission to cast them onto Him and let them pass you by! How good is that? So, stop sitting down and having a cup of tea with your anxiety! Release the need to engage, to fight or flee. But stand instead in the truth that you can trust your Saviour to take care of you.

His blood has saved not just your soul, but your mind and spirit too.

✏️ **I think that the power of communion is** instrumental in the healing journey around anxiety. It becomes a reminder to us that, because of the Cross and our surrender to it, the destroyer must pass us by.

Perhaps take some time to set up some communion for yourself and remind yourself of the story of the Cross and the power of Jesus' blood. Then before you take and partake of these emblems, I invite you to follow the process below.

I want you to imagine whatever is top of your mind at the moment—a health issue, your kids, a fear or something that has been causing anxiety in you. I want you to imagine that it is in the back of a big semi-trailer truck, and that truck is coming towards you.

I want you to picture those thoughts, those feelings, the 'what-ifs', all in that truck. It is coming towards you, and

taking a stand

the anxiety is coming towards you, and the fear is coming towards you, and you can feel the 'what-ifs' coming towards you.

What is on that truck? What are the thoughts that are associated with that fear? Is it to do with you? Is it to do with other people? Is it to do with your sense of security? Is it to do with provision?

Just let those feelings come, let those thoughts come. Just let it bubble up for a moment as that truck is coming closer.

I want you to use your imagination for a moment. What would this truck look like? What would its colour be, its size, and even its smell? And it has a name written on the side, what is that name?

That truck is in front of you, and that truck opens the door and is inviting you to sit inside and to take the wheel. The invitation is there to sit in these thoughts, mediate, and literally take this truck for a drive.

You now have a choice. Are you going to sit in this truck, turn it on, and drive off down the road of worry, fear, and anxiety? Or are you going to let that truck pass you by?

I want you to imagine there is also a train coming on the other side of you, and that train is called the Train of Life. This is a train of thoughts that brings life, hope, love, and faith. It is carried by the Spirit of God.

Imagine with me. What does it look like? What does it sound like, and what would it feel like to hop on board?

That train comes, and it stops next to you. It is inviting

you to jump in. That train is asking you to give the truck load of anxieties over to Jesus and to jump in the train of thoughts that are lovely, kind, praiseworthy, noble, and excellent. It is the Train of Life accessed by faith—faith that you can trust God will fight for you and look after you.

My point here is that you have a choice. Every day, every thought, we have a choice to jump into a truck carrying a load of anxious thoughts or give that truckload of anxieties to God and let it pass us by. Instead of getting into that truck, we can choose to get into the Train of Life activated by faith in who Jesus is. I want you to now make the choice.

You can read through Mark 14:22–24 and, when you are ready, receive your emblems and give thanks to the One who died for you.

Every day and every thought we have a choice. The truck of death or the Train of Life?

👏 **"Lord, it can be so hard not to engage when** the fear strikes, but You ask us to trust You and to trust that the blood of Jesus is enough to protect us from fear.

Lord, help us not to fight it in our strength or to run from it in our strength, but help us stand there in the mighty power of Jesus. And, Lord, when we do that, you will equip us with divine ways to fight the godly battle with godly strength and empowerment on high. In the name of the One whose blood has paid for our peace of mind, Jesus, Amen."

HIGHLIGHTS

- Where we draw our water from determines the quality of that water. This is true of our thought-lives and of the spiritual wells that we are drawing from.

- When I am working with my clients in a coaching session, I have often asked the question, "Which counsellor are you listening to in this situation? Are you listening to the counsellor of living water, or are you listening to the counsellor that has only dirty water in mind for your life?"

- The devil, who is also known as a liar, has been counselling many, if not all, of us since we were children. His ideas have shaped our worldviews, and for most of us, this has happened without us even noticing. He has shaped our perspectives on parts of our family histories, the events in our past, present, and future, and our identities.

- One of the most potent ideas that the enemy plants for those of us dealing with anxiety is one seeded in fear. Fear is the accent of the enemy, and he wields it, dominates with it, and uses it to oppress all who have come into agreement with his ideas.

- If your 'fight or flight' response is causing the fear or panic, then choosing not to run from it or fight it is actually choosing not to produce all those *Protect* chemicals and hormones. By choosing not to engage with 'fight or flight' messages, but rather choosing to accept it, we disarm the anxiety and circuit-break the fear.

- Those of us who have received Jesus as our Lord and Saviour are reminded every time we take communion, that the victory over our lives has already been fought for and won because of Jesus. His blood testifies to every power of darkness and fear that they have no power to destroy us.

- Part of spiritual warfare is simply letting dark thoughts pass us by.

- Jesus is asking you to trust Him in this process because you have the blood of Jesus on the doorways of your soul which means the destroyer of your souls is directed to pass over you. This we are reminded of every time we take communion. Perhaps you might like to partake in communion now and read Mark 14:22–24.

chapter 9

access denied

Can you remember where you were when you encountered Jesus for the first time? Who was around you at the time, and what was going on in your life that brought you to that decision? It is a powerful exercise to continually remind yourselves of how good God has been, in order to build faith in how good He will continue to be.

The Christian walk started with our surrender and continues to be one of surrender.

It is a journey of continually checking that Jesus is on the throne of our hearts and, when we find He isn't, engaging with the Holy Spirit to make that adjustment. When we don't walk in this surrendered lifestyle, other things can start to take over.

Television, work, finance, family or friends are just some of the things that we can make gods. We start bowing down to this or that and allow Jesus to be replaced as master. When this happens, the Bible calls it idolatry, and if undealt with, it can cause our lives to veer off the course of God's purpose for us. It can also open the door to spiritual consequences.

We have turned to a discussion of spiritual matters, and when dealing with the spiritual matters, it is imperative that I press the point that godly alignment is essential for spiritual health. Before any other work can or should ever be done, the first step in dealing with spiritual health is to make sure that Jesus is the King enthroned in your heart.

Surrendering to Jesus is not a one-time event—to live a life surrendered to the Father is an ongoing decision.

Before we continue, why not take a moment, and simply ask the Holy Spirit to reveal if He is currently on the centre stage of your life. If other things have crowded Him out, by the grace of God, ask Jesus to remove whatever has been your guiding force or been ruling your desires. Lay it at the foot of the Cross and invite Christ back to sit on the throne of your heart. Receive His grace and forgiveness afresh and ask to be empowered to move forward. Take some time out to do that now, and then come back to reading once you have finished.

"Jesus, I come to You humbly today and present my heart, mind, and life to Your loving care. I surrender my life afresh to You—my thoughts, the intentions of my heart, my relationship, and my life. I confess You are Master and Lord, and I give You all of who I am. Amen"

> Put on the full armour of God, so that you can take your stand against the devil's schemes. For our struggle is not against flesh and blood, but against the rulers, against the authorities, against the powers of this dark world and against the spiritual forces of evil in the heavenly realms.
> —Ephesians 6:11–12

> For though we live in the world, we do not wage war as the world does. The weapons we fight with are not the weapons of the world. On the contrary, they have divine power to demolish strongholds. We demolish arguments and every pretension that sets itself up against the knowledge of God, and we take captive every thought to make it obedient to Christ.
> —2 Corinthians 10: 3–9

Once we are in godly alignment, we are in a perfect position to deal with any demonic associations that may be at play. When we are looking at dealing with stress, anxieties, and fear, we mustn't deal only with our natural circumstances, but also take spiritual variables into consideration too.

Fear is a dialect of the enemy.
Fear can sometimes be useful but must not always be trusted.

Perhaps you are thinking, "Larissa, I believe in demonic powers, but I know we have full authority over them. So, how can the devil still impact us?"

If we were having a coffee at my house right now, I would say, "I love this question, let me pour you another coffee and explain."

We absolutely have been given authority in Jesus over the devil, but we also still have free will in exercising it. To have authority and to be able to use your authority over the enemy, are two different realities. It's the difference between owning a car and knowing how to drive it versus owning that car but breaking the law in the way we drive it.

Even in God's love and under God's grace, we can make decisions that self-sabotage our spiritual freedom. There are spiritual principles we must understand in the Kingdom of God. For example, if one of my kids, who I love dearly, was convicted for murder, there will still be consequences. Similarly, in the spiritual world, within God's love and forgiveness there can still be consequences associated with our decisions.

So, before we begin wielding our spiritual swords, it is imperative we take personal accountability where necessary. Just like we need to be in godly alignment in our hearts, as we did in the last chapter, there may need to be some other changes made in your life, so that you don't find yourself back in a similar spiritual situation next month. To accomplish this, we will be looking at how we can open access points to the enemy, and how we can make spiritual agreements that have earthly consequences.

> Be angry, but do not sin; do not let the sun go down on your anger, and give no opportunity to the devil. Let the thief no longer steal, but rather let him labor, doing honest work with his hands, so that he may be able to give to those in need.
> —Ephesians 4:26–28 (RSV)

I know, I know—sin is not a popular word. In Australia, where I live, you are almost better off dropping a swear word in some churches than talking about sin. But I am a risk taker—so here goes.

I believe that sin is a position at its core that at one point we have all found ourselves in. We can get wrapped up in pointing out behaviours as evidence of a sinful life, but I think it's bigger than that. Sin is anything that separates us from the love of God—a position that every person is in, until we are rescued. And Jesus is the rescue mission, He became human, so He could find us! No wonder God hates sin.

To accept we have sin is simply to accept that we were disconnected from the life of God in an area of ours. Jesus didn't come to condemn us. If being shown you have areas of your life where God's love isn't abiding makes you feel guilt or shame, that is not the work of God in your life.

True repentance is the feeling that you've come home to a place you belong.

His conviction of our disconnection (or sin) feels more like hope! It is strength that comes to your areas of darkness, switches on a light, points you out of the mess, and strengthens you for the journey. That is what conviction of sin feels like when the Holy Spirit is at work. I believe God wants to move across our nation, and all the nations, with a tidal wave of repentance. Not a tsunami of condemnation and shame, but living water, flushing away our pain and darkness and refuelling us with His Spirit.

That is the work of the Gospel—dealing with our sin, helping us change our direction and minds, and filling us with His grace and love, in order to live differently. To live a life of holiness is not to live a life of perfection or being mastered by legalism and behaviour modification.

Holiness is simply a life committed to divine surrender.

When we engage in sin, we give the devil a foothold in our lives because sin is the devil's playground. Repentance however, is the kindness of God and not to be mocked or dismissed as unnecessary. Repentance IS JESUS HIMSELF making a way for us out of pain and darkness and into the light. Jesus is the door, and repentance is our way to activate His grace, over and over again. Sin can so easily entangle us, but because of what Jesus has done for us, we can shake it off; we can turn back to the path of life and carry on.

Repentance needs to become the church's new buzz word because repentance is the grace of God.

Another word for grace in Hebrews is kindness. Romans 2:4 tells us that it is God's kindness that leads us to repent. It is His grace that leads us to turn around, change our minds about what is real and see God's goodness. How good is that!? Without the grace of God, we can do nothing.

His love and grace are what we need to empower us to change our lives.

Now, let me be clear, I do not think repentance is condemnation. I am not suggesting a lifestyle of self-flagellation. I am talking about a life that's committed to the Holy Spirit guiding me in holiness and surrender. A life of repentance to me is a life of continually having my mind and heart changed and transformed. I remember, early on in my Christian walk the Lord was talking to me about a lifestyle of repentance, and He showed me this vision.

God gave me a picture of an area in front of the Cross,

and there were carpark spots as far as the eye could see. Each carpark had a different type of landscape in front of it. One was totally barren, another was a wild bush, some were like a wilderness, some had freshly mown grass, and some had really worn-down patches of dirt.

I believe the Lord spoke to me and said, "Look, those parts where it is wild and full of untended bushland, that represents someone's life who never engaged with the work of the Cross in their life. A person who never engages in the victory of the Cross or the sorrow that leads to repentance."

Then He showed me the well-worn spots. These dirt patches were where knees had been so often that ditches had been dug into the dirt. Jesus told me that this represents the person that is being most effective in His kingdom because they have learnt the power of a repentant lifestyle. I felt Jesus say, "They've learnt to keep coming back and receiving the life that is found in dying before the Cross and receiving my resurrection power."

We cannot live the life that God has given us to live through our own strength and with our own behaviour-modification strategies. It must be lived through the great exchange that happens only at the Cross. We must live it with a revelation that our role is to come as we are to Jesus, and in return, we will receive His power to be who He has called us to be. Unresolved sin and a life that has not been surrendered to Christ are access points for the enemy.

> Submit yourself then to God. Resist the devil, and he will flee from you.
>
> — James 4:7

What is the first directive in this Scripture? To submit ourselves to God. If you are not submitted to God, you cannot resist the devil, and consequently, he will NOT be forced to flee. Additionally, if you choose not to walk in submission to God, the devil will continue to be a hindrance in your life.

My hope is that you will find your place in front of the Cross anew today. Perhaps for the first time in a long time—or for the thousandth time. In so doing, I believe you will kneel alongside every great mother and father of the faith.

> Be sober and self-controlled. Be watchful. Your adversary, the devil, walks around like a roaring lion, seeking whom he may devour.
>
> —1 Peter 5:8(WEB)

Part of closing access points is both being surrendered to God AND living aware that the enemy is part and parcel of this Christian walk. We must not be unaware of his schemes especially around our 'Achilles heels'. It's not just sin in our lives that we need to be alert to, but also just weak areas we are predisposed too. Do you know the areas of your life where you are at your weakest? I can tell you one now—it's fear. The enemy is going to get in on that, and if he can, try to see if he can devour you in the midst of it.

Perhaps for you, it is dealing with depression or gossip or slander? Maybe it's watching really trashy television that doesn't promote godly life choices? Where are your weak spots? Know them, because the enemy does, and he will cause damage if you don't have safeguards in place.

If you can know what they are, you are one step closer to being aware of the way the enemy makes plans for your life. Let your friends know what your Achilles heels are and invite them to speak into your life if they see you starting to slip into those things. Once you are aware of the devil's tactics or the way that he fuels your natural anxiety, guess what? He has shown his hand.

Where once it was a weakness, it now becomes your strength.

Anxiety and panic were once a huge weakness for me and places for the devil to get a foothold—until I got a clue, and I started to allow them to become some of my greatest strengths. Now when anxiety comes (and it still does), it acts as a trigger for me to think, "Right, girl! My body is giving me a signal. What do I need to deal with mentally, emotionally or spiritually?"

I invite you to do the same—make a decision that, when it comes to the enemy, he may have messed with you up until this point, but no further. He will no longer mess with your life unhindered. It's within your authority to do so. I now use anxiety as a springboard into the presence of God. It is now a reminder that I need to turn to Jesus, and where it once destroyed my life, it has become the key to my deeper strength.

👏 "Jesus, I do not want to give the enemy access to my life. Wherever there has been idolatry, wherever I have put something or someone in place of You on the throne of my heart, I ask You to take it, and I invite You back into Your rightful place in my life.

Lord, where there has been sin, I repent. Lord, help me live a life full of the Holy Spirit, full of victory. I hand over the areas of my life that are not in alignment with Your holiness, and receive Your forgiveness and grace to empower me to live differently.

Jesus, where I am weak, I ask for Your strength, and I ask these things in Jesus' name. Amen."

HIGHLIGHTS

- It is important when dealing with spiritual matters that you are in godly alignment; that Jesus is the King enthroned in your heart. Why not take a moment and simply ask the Holy Spirit to help you make Jesus the King of your life again?

- When we are looking at dealing with stress, anxieties, and fear, it is important to know that the enemy can play in the background because fear is the devil's accent. Fear is like the signature move of the devil, but we have authority over him. Remember that although fear is useful at times, it cannot always be trusted.

- There are times however, when the enemy may be present because we have given him access. The access points that we discussed in this chapter were:

    1. Sin and ignoring the grace given to us all to remain surrendered and repent.

    2. Not being alert to him and failing to ask God to open our spiritual eyes.

- Where anxiety was once a trigger for hopelessness and thoughts of dread, in Jesus, anxiety can turn us to God. Where once it was a weakness, anxiety can now become a strength.

chapter 10

the sweetest victory

✈ **Safety Instructions: This chapter speaks about abuse so, if this is a trigger for you, please be advised you might like to just skip to the end and read the highlights section.**

In the previous chapter, I introduced you to the idea of access points for the enemy. This is a very important piece of the 'being spiritually free' puzzle. I have seen many good Christians under demonic oppression because they are leaving doors of access open in their lives.

Continuing along with our journey, we will now turn our attention to the idea of forgiveness. This is always an easy thing to preach, but it can be very hard to conquer.

I have learnt though, that holding onto bitterness is like putting yourself in jail and giving the devil the key.

I would say that although the road to forgiveness has

been a very long one for me, it is also the sweetest of all victories to date. In discussing the power of choosing forgiveness, I would like to share some more of my story with you.

It would be safe to say that in every season of my life, the Lord has challenged me to forgive. Whether in relationships that turned a little sour, under leaders who treated me unkindly or when dealing with those whom I let push my buttons, forgiveness has been necessary.

Through every season though, I found that one person would rise again and again in my prayer time that I needed to forgive. With every season of life that I lived, so would come new awareness that fresh forgiveness would need to be applied to the man who had molested me.

It is true, that often kids who find themselves in abusive relationships through their formative years don't completely comprehend the impact until later in adulthood. How are they to know any different if this is their baseline? If they are being told this is what love looks like, for example, what is their reference point? This was certainly true for my life. This fractured relationship caused such deep foundational breaks in my identity that, even today, I am still impacted—but no longer destroyed—by it.

After about a decade of actively walking in forgiveness for this person, I remember saying in frustration one day, "I've already forgiven him, God. Do I have to go over this again?" In looking back now, I can see that every time God was asking me to forgive, He was in fact, taking me deeper into dimensions of who I was and the pain that I was carrying.

I can, hand on heart, say that at each season I had genuinely forgiven him. Every opportunity given in church services around forgiveness, I was on it. After every family gathering where I would have to see him, I would leave convulsing in tears but engaged in forgiving him. I remember taking communion on several occasions as a declaration to my soul that I was choosing to forgive. I was committed to being free, but like many things in God, some works take many seasons to dig down into the deeper layers, in order to be works of completion.

I sit here today though, knowing at my core I have forgiven this man. I have no ill will, no triggers or feelings of pain associated with him. My heart is free, and with it, all the baggage that I carried relating to him is gone. It is an amazing place to be, to know that neither he nor the enemy has a hold on my secrets or my shame relating to the abuse, anymore. But it was a very difficult path to walk.

I remember the day I felt a physical lifting in my heart, and a life changing freedom come over me. I was coming home from a church service and had been contemplating my early years of life. I was remembering the pain of what had transpired in my childhood, and the coverup that had taken place in my adult years. I was seeing with fresh eyes this life of lies, and how I had played along. It felt like a house of cards falling, and it became very clear what that relationship was—and what it was not.

I began crying from a place I had not known in a long time and had to pull the car I was driving over. My body became disabled as I saw the truth of my life in a way I never had before. If I had seen this even a year previously, I'm not sure I would have gotten back up, but God had made me ready for this moment. He had walked me through two decades of forgiveness, layer by layer, and built into me two decades of learning about the power of forgiveness and the grace of God for even the hardest truth. He had prepared me for this day, and I knew what I needed to do.

In a flood of tears, I asked the Holy Spirit to help me do what needed to be done. I had to forgive this man who had damaged my life so severely. This relationship lasted for years, and it has affected my marriage, my parenting, how I lived my life with anxiety and uncertainty, and how I related to God. My anxieties were born from hiding this secret and learning to not trust my own gut instinct. The agony of this all slowly moved from feeling wounded, to being very, very, very ticked off. The rage that followed was nothing short of murderous.

This is an important step—you can't forgive what you don't acknowledge.

I felt the Lord say, "If this man was here now, what would you want to say?" I spent an hour imagining that man was in the car with me. I told this imaginary passenger

the sweetest victory

everything his actions had cost me over my 40 years on the planet. I was full of unbridled rage and disgust, and even though the perpetrator wasn't there, I wasn't alone. I could feel Jesus was right there with me, taking it all in.

After I had let loose, I heard God say, "What do you want to do with him?" In previous seasons, I would have said something far less mature. However, I have learnt over the many seasons of life that my true freedom is found only in the path of forgiveness and surrender. I knew, whatever was going to happen, I didn't want one more day being affected. So I said, "Lord, help me to forgive."

It was as though time stopped in my car. I was in the driver's seat, the man was sitting in the passenger seat, and before us was the reality of the Cross. I have no way to explain to you what happened next, except that Jesus is alive, and His guidance is worth following. I have only had a few times in my life where I have experienced Jesus as tangibly as I felt Him that day. I knew I was on sacred ground.

In that moment, it was as though this man and I were both before the Mercy Seat of God, and that's when it hit me. What this man and I had in common besides being united in our secret was that we were united in needing the forgiveness of God. For different things obviously, but as a sinner saved by grace, I needed the reality of the Cross in my life just as much as he did.

We both stood before the Cross; both in need of grace; both having fallen short; both missing the mark. I felt this unity with my perpetrator, and it was the work of grace. Only grace enabled either of us to access Jesus on the Cross, and it is the same for you and those that have sinned against you. That day, something deep was healed and restored in my heart. From that day until this day, my heart towards this man is soft and free.

Forgiveness is the gift we give ourselves.

I realise for some this may seem too mystical, but it is my experience, and if it helps someone connect and forgive, I am willing to share it. As I sat in that car, I literally felt the weight of what this man had done to me lift. Like he and the sins committed against me just floated out of the car onto the Cross, and I was free. I am telling you—joyfully free! The laugh that erupted from the core of my being was like fresh water erupting out of a place that had only ever known darkness.

I was changed. From that day onwards, I can with my hand on my heart, witness to you that I am a new person. I see things differently. I see myself and my ideas and my worth differently. To choose forgiveness is to choose to be set free. It is the kindness and the wisdom of God. The alternative is to choose to remain in unforgiveness.

When I was 22, and first embarked on dealing with childhood trauma, I clearly remember having a demonic encounter. In it, the devil said to me that I would never get rid of his influence in my life because I would "never go where he resided." He thought that because the pain and the truth of my childhood was so devastating, I would never revisit it. And if I never looked at the secrets in my heart and shone a light on the dark truths of my history, he would be able to remain in the darkness. He was wrong.

Unforgiveness in your soul is like dirty, stagnant water that attracts flies and bugs and nastiness. Think of its alternative—beautiful, clean, fresh water. A healthy environment for fish and foliage and life. Now think of a cesspool, no avenues in and out, and an environment of muck and sickness. That is what unforgiveness is like. It is an environment that attracts the demonic. We want to make sure that we are not attracting the demonic and giving demons any access to us, right?!

We have to be bold and courageous to face some of the pain in our past. When we do though, we shine a light on the darkness, and with that, we expel the devil's influence. There is a powerful parable that I want us to look at together about unforgiveness, and it is found in Matthew 18, starting at verse 21 (NLT):

> Then Peter came to him and asked, "Lord, how often should I forgive someone who sins against me? Seven times?" "No, not seven times," Jesus replied, "but seventy times seven!"

Jesus then goes on to tell His disciples a parable about what the kingdom of heaven is like. He tells the story of a king who decides to settle his accounts with those that owed him money. One servant was brought to him who owed him millions of dollars.

That particular servant (let's call him Barry) couldn't pay back his loan to the king. The king then orders Barry, along with his wife and children and everything he owned, to be sold to pay the debt. But Barry falls down with his face to the floor and begs the King, "Please be patient with me, I will pay it all."

The king is filled with pity for him, and he releases him and forgives the debt. What a king, hey—sound familiar? Barry must have been feeling good, right? When Barry left the king however, he went to a fellow servant who owed him a few thousand dollars, and he grabbed him by the throat and demanded that he pay up.

His fellow servant fell down before him and begged for more time. "Be patient with me and I will pay it." But Barry wouldn't wait. Instead, Barry had the man arrested and put in prison until the debt could be paid in full. Bad, Barry, bad.

When some of the others had seen this, they were very upset. They went to the king and told him everything that had happened. Then the king called Barry in and said, "Evil servant! I forgave you that tremendous debt because you pleaded with me. Shouldn't you have mercy on your fellow servant, just as I had mercy on you?" Then the angry king sent Barry to prison to be tortured until he paid back his entire debt.

Here is the point that I want to make: Jesus then says, "That is what my heavenly Father would do to you, if you refuse to forgive your brothers and sisters from the heart."

If we who have been forgiven everything by our King cannot forgive those that have mistreated us, then we are Barry. We are in a prison of our own making. Yes, Jesus has forgiven us our sins, but if we are to remain free in our hearts, we must commit to forgiving others who've sinned against us. If we don't, we give an access point to the enemy to torture us. Jesus is giving us clear instructions on how to remain free—forgive from the heart out of the revelation of how Jesus forgave us first.

I believe some of you are dealing with panic, anxiety, and fear because you have a cesspool of unforgiveness in your heart that is attracting demonic forces. These forces of fear and intimidation are torturing you, fuelling the anxiety and holding you captive. **Fear is attracted to unforgiveness and bitterness.** Today I urge you, forgive from the heart and be released by the grace of God.

👐 **For this prayer time, I want you to sit and** give yourself time to search your own heart. Ask the Holy Spirit to show you anywhere that bitterness and unforgiveness still abide. Let events and people come to your mind and simply say out loud that you forgive them, and hand them over to Jesus in faith.

Perhaps like me, you need to imagine the person is in the room, and you need to tell them how their actions have affected you. This is not an exercise where you ring someone and tell them at this stage you forgive them. Jesus may or may not lead you to do this. This is about letting the bitterness go, so the grace of forgiveness can come and abide in your heart and bring you peace.

Then you need to break off any demonic oppression or influence that was attached to the bitterness or the relationship. Don't over think it, you just need to say, "I break off any demonic influence that was connected to this bitterness or the relationship."

Recap:

1. Take time to worship Jesus for what He has forgiven you for.

2. Acknowledge the person that has hurt you.

3. Allow yourself to enter into the pain and be honest about its effects.

4. Voice that because you have been forgiven, you will forgive.

5. Ask Holy Spirit to bring His peace and grace.

6. Break off any demonic oppression that may have been attached to the relationship and your bitterness.

HIGHLIGHTS

- In the previous chapter, I introduced you to the idea of access points for the enemy. In this chapter, we've discussed the power of forgiveness.

- I shared from my own life the power of being able to forgive the man that had molested me in my childhood. Forgiveness is the gift we give ourselves.

- Unforgiveness in your soul is like dirty, stagnant water attracting flies, bugs, and nastiness. Its alternative is beautiful, clean, fresh water—a healthy environment for fish and foliage and life. Now think of a cesspool, no avenues in and out, and an environment of muck and sickness. That is what unforgiveness is like, it is an environment that attracts the demonic.

- Read the parable found in Matthew 18:21. This explains to us that unforgiveness can bind up our hearts and bring oppression.

- Take time to work and pray through the points in the prayer section of this chapter.

chapter 11

the power of agreement

It is a profound advantage to us, when dealing with anxiety and fear, that we also have the Holy Spirit at work within us. I've worked alongside many men, women, and young adults in my secular roles over the years who've struggled with debilitating anxiety. I've been able to give them lots of skills and tools to combat their struggles, and I have seen it have a big impact, but it's not complete. Being unable to impart the transforming power that comes with knowing Jesus and His Holy Spirit is like giving them a car without an engine.

What you have, if you have the Holy Spirit, is everything you need to navigate the road before you.

If you hadn't worked it out yet, I am a proud Australian Pentecostal Christian woman. That means besides many other nuances, I believe that the gifts of the Holy Spirit that were poured out at Pentecost in the Book of Acts are still available to all believers today. Gifts such as the potential for miraculous healing, experiencing an infilling of the Holy Spirit, being able to speak in a language of the Spirit, the ability to speak prophetic words from God, and being able to deal with demonic forces—these are all ways I believe God still works in our daily lives—dynamic, hey!

In the last few chapters, I've discussed how we can give access to the demonic world into our lives in different ways. These chapters, I see as a spiritual spring clean for the body, mind, and soul. Each chapter in this section of the book will take us deeper into the house of who we are, giving us tools to ultimately be able to correct even our foundations.

In the next chapter, I will look at the very important aspect of our spiritual lives, which is understanding our authority as Christians. Before we can go more broadly into the world of spiritual warfare, however, I believe we need to go a little deeper. To do that, I think it is important to have a quick recap of the last few chapters.

Firstly, we looked at sin as an access point which we can give the devil into our lives. Perhaps in your circumstance, the sin is pride or something sexual in nature? It might be gossip or it could be that you are hearing the voice of God direct you in a certain way and you are being stubborn to His direction. The point is that, whether it seems obvious to you or not, if you have sin in your lives and are being resistant to Jesus, you are opening yourselves up to demonic influence.

Will you be oppressed by a demonic spirit? I am not

sure, because each person's circumstances are unique. I do, however, believe that if you are consciously engaging in sin, you are opening yourself up to the possibility of demonic influence over your life and living from a place that will not produce life.

Secondly, I discussed the importance of staying alert to the enemy. Not fearful—but awake! I love my country, we have the best beaches, sporting teams, culture, food, and people. Something that's not so great though, is that we also have the highest rate of skin cancer in the world. Due to my very Irish skin and extensive family history of skin cancers, I should have been getting regular skin checks most of my life. I didn't though.

I had a multitude of reasons for not being vigilant, but really none of them were very good. So, at the age of 42, after my Mum's umpteenth skin cancer removal, I went for my first ever check-up. Unsurprisingly, after inspection, a mole turned out to be cancerous. After its removal, the consequence was a big ugly scar on my back. But it could have been much worse, and I learnt a valuable lesson. Being nonchalant about cancer wasn't a smart strategy.

Being unaware of the enemy is not a smart strategy.

Just staying apathetic to his reality is only going to hurt you in the long run because he does exist. And like my cancer, he loves apathy. Left unchecked and allowed to just remain in the shadows of your life, the devil can take the unfair advantage, and that will cause unnecessary harm. Yes, you have been given full authority in Jesus to deal with him, but to do that you must stay alert to his agenda.

Finally, in the last chapter, we discussed how walking a path of forgiveness offers freedom against the enemy's snares, which for me was the sweetest victory. Choosing to forgive is how we disengage with demonic agreements. Being bitter or holding onto hurt are all examples of coming into agreement with darkness. Choosing to forgive is how we disengage from that relationship. Can you see that closing access to the enemy in your life starts with taking personal responsibility?

True spiritual warfare is won in your own heart first.

I am all for going into war against the enemy. There are times where we must demonstrate our godly authority with declarations, prophetic decrees and demonic rejections; with spiritual intercession that storms heaven, binds demonic strongholds, and rebukes devils. But if we keep access doors open to him, how effective will that actually be?

There are spaces and times in God that we must go to war, rebuking and rejecting the work of the enemy over our lives, our family, our churches, and communities, and I am all for it. However, we have to ensure in the first place that we aren't giving access to the enemy. Otherwise, we will be back where we started, next month.

I believe we have powerful saints who are going to war for churches and communities while being spiritually destroyed in private and not knowing why. The why, my friend, is because they aren't closing access points. In this chapter, I'd like to continue to build upon the idea of personal responsibility around access points by taking the idea a step further and that is the power of agreement.

> Whatever I 'align' myself with are the very things that will create a 'line' into my future.
> —Craig D. Lounsbrough

If I looked at you, face to face, on a good day and said, "Hey my friend, did you know you are actually a wombat?" There is a good chance you would think, "I am not a wombat, but there is something wrong with her." Also, if you are not Australian you might think, "Woman, what is a wombat?" It's an amazing Australian marsupial that looks like a big log with legs—but I digress.

In this interaction, you have chosen not to agree with me. You have not made an agreement with the idea being presented to you. Your internal world has listened to the incoming messaging; you have weighed it as incorrect, and you have rejected it (hopefully ☺) because you know you are not a wombat.

Our internal belief systems have been formed over time to permit or reject incoming messaging, depending on what we determine as true or false information. If I looked at some of you and said, "Hey loser, you are fat, ugly, and will never get married", some of you will have the same reaction as the wombat comment. You will brush it off because you are okay, and that the incoming messaging from me is incorrect.

Some of you, however, will hear this, weigh it up and, because it agrees with your internal belief system about yourself, will take that information, accept it, and make an agreement with it.

It was the same information, but the difference was the agreement.

Our role as sons and daughters of God is to agree with heavenly truths and to reject those which are contrary, especially when our belief systems collide. It is in so doing that we sanctify our own minds, renewing our thoughts and taking into captivity ideas that are going to oppress us. It is in capturing opinions and worldviews that raise themselves up against the knowledge of God and casting them down that we fight the good fight of faith. If we can agree with the Kingdom of God in our minds, we bring heaven to earth! But, if we can bring heaven to earth by what we agree with, it stands to reason we also can make agreements with demonic ideas.

Our spiritual agreements have earthly consequences.

Let's take an example from our last chapter. When I chose to forgive the man who sexually abused me over all those years, when I chose to come into alignment with God's guidance for my life, I came into agreement with heaven. That allowed heaven free access to flow into my life, my mind, my body, and out into every area of my life connected to this relationship. The light came and freedom flowed.

When I was not walking in forgiveness, I was ultimately, even subconsciously, holding onto undealt-with pain, shadows of hurt, and bitterness. This, in a word, is not forgiveness, this is not agreement with God's direction. And therefore, it is making an agreement that there is a better way to deal with all that pain—to hold onto it, to pretend it doesn't hurt or pretend it doesn't exist or, for you, it might be anger or revenge. All these coping strategies are agreements with ideas of dealing with life outside God's design.

Ungodly agreements attract ungodly influences.

This isn't about passing judgment on you, but about helping you to see that we make agreements with ourselves and with the world, all the time. What we need to do is to ensure that those agreements are in line with the Kingdom of God and, when they aren't, to understand that they are demonic ideas, no matter how well-intentioned. When we come into agreement with ideas from the evil one it actually causes us to come out of Kingdom alignment and out of divine order.

> This day I call the heavens and the earth as witnesses against you that I have set before you life and death, blessings and curses. Now choose life, so that you and your children may live.
> —Deuteronomy 30:19

Eve, in the Garden of Eden, is a great example of how this works. We are at the very beginning of time when all the world was in Kingdom harmony and at the precipice of the fall of humanity (insert menacing music please). She is standing at the tree, the serpent alongside her, and Eve takes her first bite of that piece of fruit and then gives it to Adam, and, at that moment, all hell breaks loose.

There is a colossal rip from divine order in her body, her relationships, her source of provision, her community, and ultimately her relationship with God.

They were disconnected from Kingdom alignment because they came into agreement with ideas outside of God.

Adam and Eve chose not to be in agreement with

God's direction which was, "Don't eat of that tree", and into agreement with the counsel of the evil one who said, "Did God really say you couldn't eat of that tree?"—and the rest, as they say, is history.

The devil is empowered by our agreements.

Over the years, the enemy has come to us—in our vulnerable times, our sad times, our times of illness, trauma, fear, anxieties, sin, apathy, pride, and he has whispered ideas to us, like he did to Eve, willing us to come into agreement with him.

If the Holy Spirit is the Great Counsellor, then it is fair to say the devil is the Toxic Counsellor! Here are some ways demonic agreements might show up in your life (not always):

- Worry, anxiety, and fear
- Torment
- Pride
- Rise in the flesh
- Addiction
- Abuse
- Occult

- Sexual perversion
- Sin
- Unforgiveness and bitterness
- Self-hatred
- Depression and other mental health challenges
- Financial issues
- Barrenness in any form (e.g., becoming pregnant, being single but deeply desiring marriage)
- Illness
- Unrighteous anger
- Presence of ungodliness, darkness, and oppression.

If you are dealing with any of these or other toxic issues in your life, ask yourself this question: is this issue evidence that I have been listening to the Toxic Counsellor?

Breakthrough is on its way!

Before we knew Jesus, the enemy played us, oppressed us, controlled and, for some, even possessed us. As believers though, under the blood of Christ and the victory won on the Cross, we no longer need to live as slaves. But that, my wonderful friends, still requires us to live in Kingdom alignment. Christianity does not abdicate us from a life of personal responsibility, and true freedom requires us to take stock of what we are in agreement with.

As I mentioned, often agreements made with the Toxic Counsellor happened in times of pain when we were hurting. The Bible referred to this in the case of Jesus as "an opportune time".

> When the devil had finished all this tempting, he left him until an opportune time.
> —Luke 4:13

If Jesus had opportune times, we will have them too, and like Jesus, we need to know how to deal with the enemy when this happens. In the next chapter, I will prepare you for the battle ahead, but in this chapter, I wanted to give you the tools for the battles that we have already faced and are now maybe reaping the consequences of.

Ultimately, the devil is just a squatter. He will find places and spaces to exist, to cause anarchy, until such time as someone with authority moves him along. We are about to move him along, but if, at a deeper level, you are in agreement with him and his ideas on forgiveness, pride or sin, then the freedom you are about to experience may be short lived. If you've taken in his toxic counselling on your worth, identity, and purpose in life, then we can rebuke him, but he will simply come back and reconnect at a more opportune time (Luke 4:13).

Next, I have given you an activity to do. It will take you some time, because this task is about agreements we have potentially made as far back as childhood. I have had to renounce agreements that I've made about finance, marriage, womanhood, friendship, and so many other things, right up into my forties! I have no doubt that I will continue rejecting ideas that come from the Toxic Counsellor from my childhood until the day I die, but they are less powerful every season. This is the process of sanctification.

I must make a very important point at this stage. This whole task cannot and must not be done out of the fear that if you don't get every agreement fixed, then the devil's going to get you! It isn't like that at all. God's grace doesn't work like a tightrope. He covers us, He holds us where we deserve judgment, and protects us where we are exposed. He is on our side in this. The idea here is not to cause you to be driven into a 'works-not-grace' mindset of having to get all your ducks in a row to 'be free'.

Jesus alone sets us free!

He does, however, want us to work on what is in our hands and become aware of agreements—the ways we make connections with the enemy are important to know. Those ideas that are accessible, that we are conscious of, that we engage in and are aware of, they are the ideas that matter in this season.

the power of agreement

I have won a multitude of battles in God—even though that deeper pain related to my relationship with the paedophile was unresolved. I saw people set free; I won people to Jesus. I was a pastor in a flagship church in our nation, and God did not condemn me because I hadn't yet been ready to deal with deeper issues of the heart. That is grace.

The Holy Spirit walked me through season by season, layer by layer, and I invite you to take the pressure off and allow God to do the same for you. My heart in sharing what I am is to help frame a worldview, but one that, at its core, must be founded on the leading of the Holy Spirit and not just a spiritual formula.

Spiritual alignment is so powerful when directed by the Creator. When God does it, like a chiropractic adjustment, Kingdom life can flow through the body! Where once anxiety was fuelled, peace can flow. That is both true for the individual and for a church community. When a community comes into unity around spiritual agreements, aligned with Kingdom agenda, whole towns can be won, and spiritual wickedness can be bound and rejected. That is the birthplace of revival.

> Truly I tell you, whatever you bind on earth will be bound in heaven, and whatever you loose on earth will be loosed in heaven.
>
> —Matthew 18:18

Are you ready to do some agreement realignment?

Think of an area in your life where you're currently not feeling like you're living in the victory of God. As you have come to this book because of your anxiety related issues, perhaps pick something you are having major stress or anxiety about at the moment. It may be childhood memories, identity concerns, marriage, career, spirituality, sexuality, health, children or being a parent, mental health or something else. Ask yourself the following questions:

1. What do you currently believe to be true about this situation?

2. What do you believe to be true about the part you play in this?

3. How do you believe you are being impacted by this?

4. What are you not getting in this that you feel you need/want?

5. What do you believe about the world and our place in it regarding this?

6. What lies from the enemy might you be coming into agreement with around this issue? List them, mind map them, pour them out, as many as you can get.

7. Look at all the thoughts you have written down and

circle which ideas echo the person of Jesus. That is, which ideas from all that you have written down above demonstrate love, hope, restoration, grace, personal maturity, personal discipline or the Cross?

8. What do you think is at the heart of this issue?

9. What do you think you are believing about yourself, about God, about others, that has come from the Toxic Counsellor?

10. Now, we are going to ask that the Holy Spirit would bring His guidance to this situation. Allow yourself some quiet time, and ask God to give you a picture, a word, a memory, a Scripture, a sound, a song or something that would indicate to you what God would want to say to you about this issue. Trust He wants to talk to you. If you struggle with this, it can help to simply put on a worship song and sit in quietness, and let the song wash over you as you ask God to speak into this issue.

"Jesus, I break agreements made with the enemy and disconnect from all the influence that has come from that alignment. I turn toward you and ask that I align now with your counsel for my life. Amen"

What about going a little deeper? I would like you to ask yourself perhaps a deeper question if you feel like this issue is either reoccurring in nature or if the feelings themselves come up for you often. I would like you to think back to a time when you can first remember feeling/thinking this way in your younger years. Don't rush it—you don't have to try to push it—trust that the Holy Spirit brings things to light in the right time.

✏️ **Now, journal through this process, and it is** important that you don't come to this process as an adult looking backward—try and get into the feelings you had as a kid. This can be done by trying to remember where you were, what you were wearing, and what was around you at the time.

1. Think back to your earliest memory related to this issue.

2. What was happening at the time of the event?

3. As that child, what do you wish people knew?

4. How do you wish things had worked out?

5. How did things actually work out?

6. What did you believe to be true about life at this time?

7. What did you believe to be true about your worth,

value, ability, etc., at this time?

8. What did you believe to be true about who you were in relation to this issue at this time?

9. Knowing what you know about who Jesus is and reflecting on the Cross and the love of Jesus you know to be true, what did you believe from the Toxic Counsellor at this time? Write everything that comes to mind, feelings, memories, ideas, thoughts—all of it.

10. What would you, as an adult looking back at your younger self, have told yourself back then?

11. Is there anyone you need to forgive?

12. Now, I want you to pray and sit and wait—and ask God to give you a picture, a word, a memory, a Scripture, a sound, a song or something that God would want you to know about this issue. If you struggle with this, it can help to simply put on a worship song and sit in quietness. Let the song wash over you, and ask God to speak into this issue.

13. Now write down what you feel/think/imagine Jesus would want you to believe about this issue moving forward.

👏 **"Father, I break every agreement I have** made in the darkness of my life with the enemy. I renounce all connections I have made knowingly or unknowingly. [Tell Jesus the agreements you have listed above in your exercise].

I repent and turn from living life under these agreements. Because of Your death on the Cross and Your blood, I cut all ties with all demonic forces from my past through to my present. In faith in the person of Jesus, I believe this to be done.

Now God, I listen to the truth of what You say about me, my life, my past, present, and future. I release Your truth bathed in grace into this area in my heart, soul, and mind. [Speak out what you feel the Holy Spirit has said to you in the exercise above]. In Jesus' name, Amen."

HIGHLIGHTS

- To be honest, this chapter really is worth the read. It will help give you a healthy, well-balanced and powerful worldview around personal breakthrough over spiritual oppression.

- Thank me later. ☺

chapter 12

your divine authority

> And these signs will accompany those who believe:
> In my name they will drive out demons ...
> —Mark 16:17

I was in the throes of my mental breakdown in 2014, and I had been trying all the different strategies and tools we've been talking about thus far. I was starting to feel shifts in my thinking, my body, and my soul, but I knew I still had a way to go. As I was listening to a sermon one day, it occurred to me that, with all the things that I had been doing, I hadn't been taking authority over my situation.

Yes, I had worship music playing all the time—and I mean all the time, in every room of my house, 24-hours a day—but, in terms of taking authority over the devil, I hadn't been doing anything. It was like a light bulb went on. I had been dealing with the anxiety from a natural angle (which is necessary), but I hadn't been walking in spiritual freedom.

In that moment, I simply stood to my feet, and I took authority over the spirit of fear and intimidation. I bound those influences and rebuked them in Jesus' name and felt something lift off me instantly. A heaviness I hadn't even realised I had been carrying just evaporated.

From that day until today, I have felt a shift over my life around dealing with fear. There was a seismic change in my everyday life because I simply woke up, became alert, and took authority over the spirit of fear and intimidation. It was like a veil of fear that hung around me vanished, and I regained a sense of empowerment for my situation. I could see clearly to move forward.

Was everything perfect? Of course not. Was walking in freedom a daily journey? Of course, it was. Were there more big shifts to come? Yes, but this was a huge leap forward. We must be active in the good fight if we are to benefit from what Christ has won for us. We need to be alive and awake to the spiritual world that we are a part of if we are to walk in victory.

You might ask why God didn't just have me take authority from the very beginning? The answer is, in part, why I also waited till toward the end of the book to discuss spiritual authority. Sometimes, God needs to do a level of healing and transformation internally before we are ready to be externally free.

It is possible to get so fixated on external spiritual freedom that we forsake the internal

transformation that is <u>required to remain free</u>.

Many people are praying off external spiritual strongholds, but their internal framework, beliefs, and thoughts are still ungodly and not aligned with Kingdom truth. Now, let me stress, there is so much grace for this process, and demons are not capable of jumping on every believer's agreement. It is however something that, over time, can become a foothold and therefore worth keeping a check on.

> When an impure spirit comes out of a person, it goes through arid places seeking rest and does not find it. Then it says, "I will return to the house I left." [25] When it arrives, it finds the house swept clean and put in order. Then it goes and takes seven other spirits more wicked than itself, and they go in and live there. And the final condition of that person is worse than the first.
>
> —Luke 11:24–26

Let me state for clarity, I don't believe a Christian can be possessed by a demon. I do however believe that the Bible teaches us that Christians can be oppressed by demonic influences. Should this frighten us? No, that is absolutely not what the Bible teaches us. It teaches us that we need to be awake to the enemy. And that starts with acknowledging his reality. We need to be aware of his agenda and be confident that we walk in the victory of Christ concerning him.

Let this be your reminder to keep your eye out for the enemy.

It's my opinion that spiritual warfare is neither outdated or an idea that only lives in the Scriptures. It is inescapable that if you worship Jesus and are carrying out the great commission, you will come up against the demonic. It's part of a born-again, spirit-filled Christian's life experience to run up against demonic resistance. In fact, it could even be said that if you aren't engaging in levels of spiritual warfare, you aren't fulfilling your Kingdom assignment.

Did you know that around a quarter of Jesus' ministry was dealing with demonic influence? Important to note here, the people Jesus was working with in this way were the people of God. They were not nonbelievers living in a dark dungeon of witchcraft, but the Israelites, God's chosen people. If Jesus needed to deal with the devil to fulfill his purpose on earth, perhaps we might too? It's imperative to make the point that we are Jesus-lovers, and not demon hunters.

> Be sober [well-balanced and self-disciplined], be alert and cautious at all times. The enemy of yours, the devil, prowls around like a roaring lion [fiercely

hungry], seeking someone to devour.

—1 Peter 5:8 (Amp)

There are times in God where we must learn the posture of sitting. To sit in stillness receiving from God, soaking in His presence and just being. Breathing in His peace, enjoying who He is or lamenting and offloading all the trials of our day or season. We take time to share our burdens and offload the pain or frustration of life to a God that cares and listens.

These are times in God that care for our soul and bring healing or refreshment. It is in this way we, as His kids, learn to know His presence and recognise His voice. Without this connection, this intimacy with God, we're not poised or prepared for the other component of effective Christian living.

The Kingdom of God is birthed on earth, <u>not only</u> through intimacy with God <u>by receiving</u>, <u>but also</u> by pushing into the enemy's landscape and taking dominion in Christ <u>through 'doing'</u>.

Yes, there are times for soaking in His presence, and then there are times in God for getting things done. For taking authority, for commanding the devil to flee, for engaging in spiritual warfare, for preaching the gospel, for healing the sick, and for prophesying the promises of God into our lives and declaring His victory of the Cross over our lives (just to name a few).

> For we do not wrestle against FLESH AND BLOOD, but against principalities, against powers, against the rulers of the darkness of this age, against spiritual hosts of wickedness in the heavenly places.
> —Ephesians 6:12 (NKJV, emphasis added)

This well-known Scripture directs us to engage in a wrestling match, but remember it is with an enemy who has already been defeated and made a public spectacle of at the Cross. When you think of the wrestling match, don't think of it between two equal opponents, because if you do you are not viewing it correctly.

My handsome husband is 6 feet 7 inches tall. His nickname from the youth kids at church is 'Viking' (yes, he loves it). My daughters are both little and love to wrestle this Viking of a man. This is not an equal match. This is not a fair fight, and this is not a wrestle that will even be close in comparable strength. It is the same kind of wrestle as that which we are called into with powers and principalities. Jesus is the Viking in our story who demolished Satan, and Jesus lives within us.

Think of Satan like a squatter who will inhabit a space and bring influence, until a person with authority removes him.

I would love to give you some Scriptures now to mediate on. We must know our authority as Children of

God, so that we can rebuke the squatter in our lives. We must learn to rise in our authority for our children, families, and communities. We as Christians have a mandate from God to be image bearers, to be Kingdom bringers, and we cannot do this if we don't walk in godly authority when we are faced with a wrestling match. And remember, we wrestle from a place of victory!

Quick Note: It is not for us to restructure demonic spiritual activity when it comes to the structure of Hades. Our role, our delegated authority, has boundaries to it. We have been given authority when it comes to matters of the earth. When the devil is bringing influence into the earthly realm, we are able to engage in the Spirit and remove him when instructed to by Jesus to do so.

We do not send the devil to hell, for example, or try to dismantle his reality or existence. That is not in our realm of authority. There will be a time when the devil is finally dealt with, but that is not our fight. Ours is to be 'in Christ' and allow Jesus within us and through us, to reject the enemy when it comes to him and his presence on the earth. A great book that helps with the distinction is *Needless Causalities of War* by John Paul Jackson.

Below you will find Scriptures on our authority. Take some time to read them. These are true for all those who have accepted Christ as their Lord and Saviour. Perhaps find a place you can be alone, pop on some worship music, and begin to declare these into your situation.

- The Spirit who lives in you is greater than the spirit who lives in the world.

  —1 John 4:4b

- Behold, I have given you authority to tread on serpents and scorpions and over all the power of the enemy and nothing shall hurt you.

  —Luke 10:19

- On this rock I will build my church and the gates of hell will not prevail against it. I will give you the keys to the kingdom of heaven and whatever you bind on earth shall be bound in heaven, and whatever you loose on earth shall be loosed in heaven.

  —Matthew 16:18–19

- And these signs will accompany those who believe: In my name they will cast out demons.

  —Mark 16:17

- The Spirit of God, who raised Jesus from the dead, lives in you. And just as God raised Christ Jesus from the dead, he will give life to your mortal bodies by this same Spirit living within you.

  —Romans 8:11

- For the weapons of our warfare are not of the flesh but have divine power to destroy strongholds.
  —2 Corinthians 10:4

- Then you will know the truth, and the truth will set you free.
  —John 8:32

- So, if the Son sets you free, you are free indeed.
  —John 8:36

We must walk in our authority if we are to fulfil the mandate of God on our lives. The enemy loves nothing more than to bring strife to Christians who don't know their authority. He is in our playground, we are NOT IN HIS, but we must be sure not to give him any access as we walk in our authority. I urge you to give him his marching orders in Jesus' name.

Let's get active now and pray together.

👏 "**Lord, I ask You to come and empower me** to activate the authority that You have given me. Where the enemy is bringing fear, anxious thoughts, worry or intimidation, help me now to rebuke him in Your name. You have given me weapons that are divine, and in faith, I will use them."

I want you to stand up and speak this out loud with faith.

"Where the spirit of fear and intimidation has come against me, I take authority in the name of Jesus, and I rebuke you. You will lift off your oppression from me because of the authority Jesus has given me. I reject you and believe right now that the anointing of Christ breaks the yoke."

Now worship and begin to tell Jesus all the ways you love Him.

"Thank you, Lord, we are so grateful that You saved us and found us. That You stayed with us and haven't left us. We are so grateful that in the midst of our greatest trials You are with us, holding us, helping us, and empowering us. Thank you for Your anointing, and thank you for Your Holy Spirit that teaches us and guides us.

Presence of God, we invite You into this space and yield to You completely. We are conscious of Your greatness, that You are far above every power and principality, and that we too are seated with You in heavenly places.

We thank You right now that You are our God, and You have chosen us to be Your children.

In the mighty name of Jesus Christ. Amen."

HIGHLIGHTS

- Let me state for clarity, I do not believe either I or any born again Christian can be possessed by a demon. But I do believe the Bible teaches us that Christians can be oppressed by demonic influences. Should this frighten us? No.

- 'Be sober [well-balanced and self-disciplined], be alert and cautious at all times. The enemy of yours, the devil, prowls around like a roaring lion [fiercely hungry], seeking someone to devour.'

  —1 Peter 5–8 (Amp)

- As Christians, it is our responsibility to understand our authority in Christ, so that we can activate the Kingdom to come into our lives and to deal with the enemy accordingly.

- Think of Satan like a squatter who will inhabit a space and bring influence until a person with authority removes him.

- Read through the Scriptures I have provided on your authority and then get to work!

chapter 13

soul arise

We are nearing the end of our deactivating journey together. However, this is not the end of the road for you, or for me, but in many ways just the start of the next chapter of life. As we move now into the final parts of the book, I would like to spend the rest of our time together, giving you the tools you will need to go deeper into where your anxieties may be coming from, so that everlasting change is truly possible.

When I first came to Lord, I would spend hours every day in my room communing with the Holy Spirit. He would wash me with His love and grace and teach me about His presence. I was learning how to hear the Holy Spirit speaking to me and being immersed in prophetic experiences. He was unveiling certain things that HE had in store for my life. To this day, I look back and see so many events that have happened in my life that were foretold back in that room.

This was also a season of healing, where I discovered God as the great Counsellor. He would carefully uncover deep pains and traumas of my past and teach me how to bring these places of my heart and mind to Him. Learning to receive His life in place of my brokenness in those days set me up for the journey of sanctification that was to come. Although I gave my life to Jesus at 21, the giving over of my life is a continual process that has taken place in every season of my life.

It's not been an easy process though. Each new season of life would bring up issues from my past. I remember thinking, "seriously, how many times do I have to forgive? Or, "how many years does it take to be over this?" In response, the Holy Spirit would always whisper the same thing to me:

"Daughter, we are not starting all over again, but instead, we're digging deeper into who you are."

Many of us came to Christ later in our stories with complex histories to unravel. And even if you grew up as a Christian, I'm yet to find someone with a perfect story. Growing up in a sinful world comes with ideas, beliefs, and an identity that has been forged, at least in part, outside of God's design.

Part of the deactivation of our anxiety, then, is to engage in divine transformation. Which includes inviting God into all of who we are, including our childhood. I began writing about the importance of this in a previous chapter and now we will take more time to cover this important step in deactivating anxiety. For some of you reading this section this may not feel relevant. If that's you and you feel that God's life is soaked deep into your childhood, then I invite you to move to the next chapter. For the rest of us, I am going to offer some thoughts on being fully integrated, which means Jesus is immersed in all of who you are.

Safety Instruction: Over the next two chapters we are going to be discussing childhood wounds and the deeper places of who we are. If your childhood is a sensitive topic or a trigger for trauma, please speak to a health professional before proceeding.

God loved us when we were kids, just as much as He loves us now. Our hurts, failings, and disappointments were as important to Him back then as they are today. I do not believe that God wipes out our past from His memory just because it may have been before we were saved.

The sin may have been forgiven, but the soul was treasured.

Our childhood is part of who we are, and God wants it to be a place where you are able to look back and see He was with you then as much as He is now. As I said, I think it would be a rarity to have come through childhood completely unscathed. You may not have had parents' divorce or have experienced sexual abuse but most of us had pain, loneliness, bullying or some other experience that wounded us. Some much worse than mine. That means that, unless you have invited God into these wounds, these events may still carry a place of pain in your soul—even as an adult.

I believe childhood wounds can be seeds, and as adults, those seeds could now be bearing toxic fruit.

Anxiety can be one of these fruits. When we were kids, the logical rational part of our brains had yet to be developed. If you experienced trauma therefore, or if you experienced anything as a kid that caused you to be highly stressed or fearful, guess what part of the brain you utilised? Your stress response, your 'fight or flight' response, or what we define as your *Protect* messaging. You didn't have access to rational or logical strategies as yet because that front part of your brain hadn't even developed!

As a child, you drew from your *Protect* messaging system to cope with painful experiences.

Interestingly, as an adult when you are in 'fight or flight' mode, the entire rational part of the brain shuts down. It does this so that the 'fight' or 'flight' response or what I have termed the *Protect* messaging can pump hard through your system. This allows you to be fully alert and able to respond to threats or triggers. What it doesn't allow for however, is for you to make strong logical decisions.

Here is the interesting part (in case you were getting bored): As adults, if we've never learned new coping strategies for stressful situations, we will go back to the old strategies that we came up with as children. This means that, although we have the resource in our minds to think clearly and logically today, we choose instead to revert to our *Protect* messaging. It is like our default mode of coping.

We do this because that is the pattern of thinking we have developed since childhood.

Many of us are walking around as fully-grown adults using coping strategies that have somewhat matured but really were developed in our younger years. What do we do about this? I believe we come up with new tools and deactivators for our stress. We use the tools in this book to come up with adult strategies to replace the childhood ones.

Another easy deactivator then is to actively switch on the logical part of our brain (thus deactivating the *Protect* messaging). We can begin to do this by knowing what is happening. We can simply say to ourselves during anxiety, "Thank you, *Protect*, but I don't need you now. I'm an adult, and I desire to cope with this situation using adult coping strategies. I invite logic into this situation." By doing this, we are actually helping to switch off the 'flight or fight' response and switch on our logic.

That is a simple new tool. But what about the

memories of our childhood that caused us to go into 'fight or flight' mode in the first place? That is where I turn for the next two chapters. It's my goal to help you find God's grace and God's healing in your childhood afresh and anew. We want to be integrated with 'all' of who we are, including our childhood. In doing so, we become fully alive and fully present. Are you ready?

In my mind, the little child in us represents the purest form of who we are. It is the seed form, the core of our souls, the conception of our gifts, talents, and identities. It is the seat of our souls, and the garden bed of our hearts.

God wants to be Lord of our childhood.

Let me just give some clarity about the land of inner healing connected to the past. There is NO need to go back into every single memory that you've had to dissect it. I don't believe that the Lord wants to unravel every part of our past to renew our minds and transform us.

I have to say, though, I do see a bit of this thinking in Christianity. I see beautiful Christian people that set up camp in this land of inner healing. I think there are certainly seasons where God concentrates more on deep healing, so I am not against the process. However, it is always because God is guiding us, and it is always in the process of growing and moving forward.

Isaiah 58 has always served as guidance in the area of inner healing for me. I encourage you to go and read it, but the highlight for me is this. We are told that it is **as we go about serving God**, promoting justice, and declaring His mercy that our healing comes.

It's **as we go about the Father's business** that He shows us areas in our lives that need refinement and renewal. He isn't bringing transformation as we sit around focusing on our inner worlds and unpacking our own lives. We don't wait to be healed to follow God, but it is in following God and the truth of His Gospel that the healing flows to us.

We are children led by the Holy Spirit.

Now that I have given some boundary lines for inner healing, let us look at how this can work. I believe that there are certain defining moments in our lives where we made vows or held onto offence, pain, unforgiveness or grief. We allowed thoughts and beliefs that are not Kingdom mindsets to enter our souls and lock in. When we did this, we came into agreement with darkness as I discussed in the chapter on the power of agreements. This creates strongholds in our thinking and perhaps even connections with demonic influences.

We can identify this because we have ungodly fruit in our lives, perhaps like anxiety. But the good news is that God wants to bring new life to you. To do this, the Lord will lead us at times to memories from our past where we are in darkness in order to bring His life and new freedom.

Larissa De Michiel

There are times God has us look at our past to bring freedom into our future.

I would like to share a story from Mark 5:39–42 (BSB):

> [Jesus] went inside and asked, "Why all this commotion and weeping? The child is not dead, but asleep." And they laughed at Him. After He had put them all outside, He took the child's father and mother and His own companions, and went in to see the child. Taking her by the hand, Jesus said, "Talitha koum!" which means, "Little girl, I say to you, get up!" Immediately the girl got up and began to walk around. She was twelve years old, and at once they were utterly astounded.

Every time I read this story, I see more than just a girl lying on a bed. What I see is someone's crushed childhood hopes and dreams lying on that bed. I see perhaps a boy that was abused in childhood and so he died to his dream of being musical. I see the girl whose family moved year after year and she couldn't make friends, so she died a little to dreams of friendship.

Perhaps it's a boy that was bullied about his creativity, a girl neglected and so dead to romantic relationships or someone who failed a subject and gave up on a career dream.

I see you, who went through something that crushed

your inner world enough that a part of you died, lying on that bed. I also see Jesus, coming to each of us in our childhoods where we felt we died. Jesus coming into our hopes and dreams, coming to minister to the innocence and vulnerability of our childhood and telling us:

This area is not dead as you suppose, merely sleeping. And I am your wake-up call.
It's time to arise.

I just want you to see yourself in your prophetic imagination, lying on your own childhood bed or somewhere you felt safe as a kid. At this point, I simply want you to ask Jesus if there is anything in your childhood He would like to minister to today.

Any area that due to a painful experience in your childhood was crushed in you—a part of who you are, a part of your God-designed identity, that you think was killed off in your childhood, and that God wants to bring back to life.

Here are some ideas

- Creativity
- Physical activity
- Friendship
- Being involved in church community

- Enjoying deep intimacy
- Humour
- Intelligence
- Expression
- Emotions
- Strength and courage
- Sensitivity
- Vulnerability
- Career aspiration
- Or whatever was crushed in your soul that is being called back out by Jesus today.

It is important that you don't rush these times of ministry and that you allow for Jesus to identify what He is wanting to minister to. There is no need to relive the experience that crushed you. The important point here is to identify what was seemingly killed off in you. Once you have identified this, you can move forward.

Now in your prophetic imagination, I want you to see yourself in this Scripture. See Jesus walking into the room, and Him taking you by the hand. Let this experience be yours. What will Jesus say to you in this time? Will you let Him come into that space in your life?

He may have a special word He wants to give you about the situation. You may get a Scripture in your heart or a picture of Jesus holding you. Let His peace come into that situation. As always, I encourage you to have some worship music playing and allow Him time. Finally, when you are feeling ready, speak over yourself, "Arise. Arise [your name] in this area of your life and use it to serve the Lord." Selah.

A final thought on the Scripture. This little girl didn't have faith—not a scrap of it. She was dead! She didn't have a plan for healing. She didn't do a 21-day fast to activate her faith, again. She was out cold. It was Jesus and the faith of the people around her that caused her to live again.

You might find yourself in a similar place with your anxiety. Perhaps you have lost the faith that you will ever get better. If that sounds like you, then let me encourage you—this girl did not have that faith and yet Jesus still found her, and He will find you too. This book is my faith for you! I pray that, just as the faith of Jesus and the parents and the disciples brought healing to that little girl, this book and my faith will do the same for you, if you need it.

HIGHLIGHTS

- Growing up in a sinful world comes with ideas, beliefs, and an identity that has been forged, fully or in part, outside of God's design.

- Part of the deactivation of our anxiety is to engage in divine transformation. This includes inviting God into all of who we are, including our childhood.

- When we were kids the logical, rational part of our brains had yet to be developed. So, if you experienced trauma, or if you experienced anything as a kid that caused you to be highly stressed or fearful, guess what part of the brain you utilised? Your stress response—your 'fight or flight' response.

- Here is the interesting part: As adults, if we've never learned new coping strategies for stressful situations, we just go to the old strategies that we came up with as a kid: 'fight or flight' or *Protect* mode. We do this because that is the pattern of thinking we have developed.

- Many of us are walking around as fully-grown adults, using coping strategies, that have somewhat matured but are mostly what we came up with when we were kids.

- God wants to be Lord of our childhood.

- The Lord does lead us to memories of the past to bring freedom into our future.

- **Here is an important note:** I am not talking about going back into every single memory that you've ever had or every single trauma that you've ever lived through and dissect it. We are not navel gazers.

- Jesus does want to be Lord of our childhood though and that means us inviting Him into it.

Let God lead this journey.

chapter 14

the deeper place

> Guard your heart above all else, for out of it flow the issues of life.
> —Proverbs 4:23
> (author's paraphrase)

We have turned into the last part of our journey together, and I reckon I may have saved the best for last, but it is also probably the hardest. That is, dealing with the deeper places. Proverbs 4:23 has been a huge life verse for me since I had my breakdown and a great place to start this chapter.

If it can be said that "out of your heart flow the issues of life," then we can reverse engineer this process. What do I mean? I have come to see that many issues we experience in life come from the state of our hearts. If you are dealing with issues like anxiety in your life, it is very possible there can be heart work or belief work that needs to take place to change it. Now obviously, not every issue is a result of heart issues, but it is worth the investigation.

Anxiety and fear require our courage to take the journey into our inner life.

I see my heart much like a garden that needs constant tending. Where has unforgiveness set in? Where are there weeds of discontent or bitterness? Where do I need to erect boundary fences, or where am I lacking the water and sun that brings life? Tending to our hearts is our responsibility, but it is not something Jesus leaves us to do alone.

I have been fascinated with the development of 'self' since my early teens. I'd read 'self-help' books and try and help my friends figure out their lives. Which is hilarious because I was a total mess. Since becoming a Christian however, I can see that all the work of self, unless done in conjunction with the Holy Spirit, will lack deep and lasting change.

That is why in the opening chapter of this book, you may remember that I wrote, "This is not meant to be a 'self-help' book, but a Spirit-inspired experience with Divine impartation and transformation!" I don't believe that process can be complete without going deeper into what is at the root of some of your anxiety.

In my journey of working in the welfare industry, I've discovered many different ways to support people with debilitating issues in developing a 'stronger self'. During what I describe as my 'unfinished but fruitful' degree in social work, I came across the world of life coaching. I loved many of the components of what I was learning so much that I ended up moving out of my degree and into studying coaching.

I was a case worker during this time, working with teenagers who were in respite. I began combining my theology degree, a strength-based approach from my social work degree, and the coaching I was learning. What I started to see were significant shifts in people's lives. Particularly as I added to all of this the gift of prophecy. Working with people in this way, a picture began to emerge before me of a tree with roots and fruits.

I could see that behaviours connected to addictions, depression, relationship struggles, fears, and anxieties were often the fruits of deeper issues. I could see that if I helped people dig into the deeper issues and uproot unhealthy beliefs at a foundational level, great shifts and breakthroughs were possible.

I became fascinated with belief systems—not just any belief systems—but core foundational belief systems. Specifically, ones that people hold onto that aren't in line with Scriptural, Kingdom truths. So much so that I opened my own coaching business helping Christian women! The results continue to blow me away.

Sinful behaviours are like rotten fruit. To remove them, we must dig out the roots in the heart that feed them.

To simply cut off bad fruit like anxiety, and not go on

the journey to find out what might be at the root of that fruit, means that, in time, the fruit can grow back. I have given you many tools in the book so far for dealing with your fears, and they are all required in order to rebuild a life of strength. However, if we do not also commence the task of uprooting ungodly internal root systems, the real issues will return in time.

> Do not be conformed to this world, but be transformed by the renewal of your mind …
> —Romans 12:2 (ESV)

Beliefs about relationships, being a man or woman, being a parent, who we are as humans or what we are capable of, to name just a few, can be expansive, life giving, nurturing, and faith filled. They can also be restrictive, crushing, limiting, and ultimately seeded in sinful ideas. As a Christian, I see both beliefs that are centred and formed in the life of God, and beliefs that have been forged in darkness which destroys.

The key is to identify and remove what is toxic and feed what is healthy.

We previously discussed the power of making agreements. That when we have an internal agreement in line with God's directive, it will bring life. When, however, we have agreements that are outside of Kingdom truth, it will produce a level of deformity.

the deeper place

Some ill-health may not be felt for decades. But just like a person that starts their journey just 0.000001 cm off-course, over time, will miss their destination, so too will the person whose core beliefs are off-course. I believe our beliefs evolve over time, and therefore it is imperative that the seeds of identity and the foundational beliefs at the core of who we are, are rooted in Kingdom life. Let me show you how this all works.

When we were young, we were like sponges gathering in all the activities that happened both around us and to us. We simply just took in all that happened in our worlds. As we grew into childhood, we began to ask some questions about the layers of life and subsequently began forming ideas. We asked questions from our families, cultures, and communities, like: "What is right and what is wrong?" "Who am I?" and "What does it mean to be me in this world?"

Then we head into the pre-teenage season where we start to move out of the soaking and questioning phases and into seeking external confirmations around the ideas beginning to be formed within us. The experiences we have in this stage, the relationships, and the messaging either confirm what we think is right, or they make us change our developing ideas.

Then comes the land of the teenager, and things change again in this evolution of our core beliefs. Once a person arrives here, they are no longer on a search for confirmations or denials—that phase is over. A person has by now made up their mind about foundational issues in their world. Personal beliefs become less malleable and more finite (just ask the parent of a teenager), and those core beliefs, unless deeply challenged later in life, are now cemented in the teenager's soul.

From here, we move on through life; creating experiences to match our beliefs.

This is an idea termed 'belief-dependent realism', where we match internal beliefs about life to our external experience. Let us take the example I introduced in a previous chapter 'Power of Agreement' around being called a wombat. If you recall, I suggested that, if I called you a wombat, your internal belief system would disagree with that statement. Your inner knowing would reject that as truth, but why? You rejected it because, over time, you had developed a deeper sense of who you are, right? Let's develop this idea more and dig a little deeper.

Over your lifetime, as I just described, your agreements developed into a 'knowing' about things in life or a belief of what is true and what's not. With this knowledge, you shape your community and your external world. For example, you are less likely to continue to be welcoming of me in your world if I insist on telling you, every time that we are together, that you are indeed a wombat. It is likely that you would pull away from me because, at a deeper level, I am not matching externally what you know to be true internally.

We tend to naturally reject external realities that don't mirror our internal beliefs.

Yes, the wombat is a silly example, but what about some more serious beliefs with negative consequences? Dr Adi Jaffe a world-renowned mental health expert and a lecturer at UCLA believes there are five common destructive core beliefs that people hold. These are:

1) I am unlovable,
2) I am unworthy,
3) I don't belong,
4) I am defective, and
5) I am powerless.[13]

Do you identify with any of these?

Perhaps you hold different ones, but my point remains that, if we are holding onto beliefs that are not in line with the Word of God, then we are giving structure to our lives that is based on lies. A house built on the sand, no matter how pretty will fall, in time, because its foundations are not built on the Rock (Matthew 7:24–27).

---

13   https://www.psychologytoday.com/nz/blog/all-about-addiction/201805/6-easy-ways-cultivate-positive-thinking-today?amp 1.7.2021

✈ **Safety Instructions:** We are about to take a dive into some deep and potentially triggering events. Many come to this book with deep trauma and that requires someone to support you with more expertise than I have. If you are also dealing with suicide or extreme anxiety, you must speak to your health practitioner before proceeding. Please be wise.

Let me share a personal example of how this played out for me with respect to being sexually mistreated. As a toddler, I was a sponge towards this relationship and the other factors at play in that period of my life. When asking questions related to trusting my inner voice during these years, it emerged that I was being conditioned to believe there was something wrong with me.

Between the ages of 10 and 14, I was in an intense season where my parents had just unexpectedly split up, there were some other internal and external pressures, and I was sent to boarding school. Now, my parents will have a different perspective to mine, but what is important for the sake of this process is my perception of this time. What we are looking for is *what was the story I was telling myself* during this time. What was the external confirmation I was receiving to my internal ideas that had been formulated over my childhood? The answer was that I believed I was dirty, unlovable, and unwanted.

Perhaps if I hadn't had the intense experiences

around this stage of my life, then I would have landed on a different inner core belief in my inner musings regarding who I was. However, this difficult time in my life confirmed my ideas about my identity. Subsequently during my later teenage years, I began to live in such a way that attracted experiences that matched my inner belief system.

We live our lives externally in ways that mirror our inner belief systems.

Why doesn't God just dismantle all these core beliefs at the beginning of our walk with Him? For many of us, the belief systems we have in place are giving structure to our lives. There may be unhealthy roots, and we may be up against toxic fruit, but the system is still keeping us somewhat steady.

Think of it like a strangle vine. On one hand, this vine sucks all the life out of a tree, but on the other hand is being used kind of like a support structure. If that strangle vine was simply removed all in one go, that tree, which may be starved of nutrients, will also be unable stand. Rather than removing all our beliefs and uprooting unhealthy roots in one go, Jesus does the work gradually—because He is the Master of transformation and healing.

Over my life, I have seen the Great Gardner remove fruits, stems, and roots meticulously and methodically. Even this gradual removal has at times left me almost unable to stand. I cannot imagine what would have happened if it was just done in one go, like I have often prayed. With each removal, He has allowed me to replace those toxic, decaying thought systems with new beliefs that bring me life.

Bit by bit, vine by vine, one thought, idea, concept, and belief at a time, Jesus detangles and pulls them away—until we find ourselves in a chosen season where He can remove the whole belief system by the root. When that day comes, you will need every previous season's lesson learnt to be ready for it, but what a day it is!

Every morning since I was a teenager, for example, I had woken up with this heavy feeling of dread and a deep anxiety in my stomach. My first thought when I'd become aware of the morning was, "I want to die." I'd ask other people in my life if they battled the same oppression, and they would say no. By the time I reached my late thirties, I'd just put it down to me not being a morning person, and that I would live this way for the rest of my life. Thankfully, I was wrong.

One day, when I was in a ministry session, God said He had something for me. He showed me what was like a room in my heart that I had not yet opened to Him. I opened the door on His invitation, and I had this memory flood back to me of being abused as a child. The cry that erupted out of my heart took me (and the group I was with) by surprise.

After the pain in that space had subsided, I felt Jesus say, "Look for me." Using my heart's imagination and trusting God to show me what He wanted too, I looked over and saw Jesus standing there. What impacted me was Jesus shaking His head in total disappointment at the perpetrator.

I knew in this moment exactly what Jesus was saying. I let out another deep, guttural cry as the revelation hit me. What was done to me was wrong, and I was 100% right to have felt uncomfortable, claustrophobic, and trapped. I was almost 40 years of age, had done decades of inner work, and yet still at my core I believed something was wrong with me.

Jesus flooded me with many revelations in that moment. Truths from His heart, not just clichés from a book. The most powerful of these was that even if others had used me, I mattered deeply to Jesus. I knew in my inner core that my entire life mattered to the King of the universe. I felt waves of healing enter the foundations of my identity.

From that day until this one, I have never again woken up with that dread in the morning. My claustrophobia isn't like it was; I can fly on planes and be in lifts. I was changed because I allowed Jesus to work at the core of who I am. When we allow our inner lives to be transformed with His truth, external fruits will change. Even behaviours that we wouldn't think are connected.

There is no escaping though, that great courage is required to walk the path that allows the Holy Spirit into painful places we have shut the door on. If we are to really change, however, we must allow the process to take place.

Dealing with the core of who we are, dealing with our heart issues, is key to living a healthy, 'deactivated anxiety' type of life.

> Anxiety, depression, burnout, frustration, angst, anger, grief, and so on are emotional and physical warning signals telling us we need to face and deal with something that's happened often at a deeper level. This pain, which is very real, is a sign that you are in a state of disequilibrium. It's not a sign of a defective brain. Mental health challenges are normal and need to be addressed, not suppressed or things will get worse.[14]
>
> —Dr Caroline Leaf

We must deal with the root systems of our lives, otherwise disease becomes our portion.

The question then becomes: how do we identify places where we have ungodly core beliefs that aren't bringing health? We come back to the idea I mentioned at the beginning of this chapter. We reverse engineer the issues of our lives back into our heart. When dealing with a repeated situation or pattern in our lives, it is often possible to backtrack into defining moments in our younger years where we had similar inner feelings.

---

14   Cleaning Up Your Mental Mess Dr Caroline Leaf, Baker Books, Grand Rapids, Michigan 2021 Page 498

Our beliefs, whether rooted in God or not, hold residency in our lives. They hold life or death and produce good fruit or toxic.

These places in us, these beliefs, hold agreements that are ungodly, and they need to be changed. Perhaps you need to surrender that time of your life? You may find in your investigation that you need to forgive or repent. Maybe you need to take authority over where the enemy has been causing some oppression in this inner belief? You will need all the tools I have given you through *De Activate Anxiety* in order to engage in this final exercise.

Can I say, before you proceed, there is a caution in this process. It is imperative that this is a work of God, and that we ask Him to guide us and lead us in the seasons of His planning. Let me say again, the process of transformation is not ours to manipulate or force.

Uprooting core beliefs for most will be many more years in process, and that is God's perfect timing. The exercise below will work for whatever stage you are at in detangling the vines. Whether dealing with the vines or with the roots, trust the process and let Him lead.

🖉 **I encourage you to let someone know that** you are about to embark on this journey.

Here are some questions to ask yourself to help identify beliefs related to your anxiety. This is an activity that is worth taking your time over and can be used whenever you come to a point where you need personal breakthrough.

- What is an issue I am currently facing that is causing me anxiety?
- What are the thoughts associated with the anxious experience?
- What are the common thoughts I have that are self-destructive and defeating?
- What do I tell myself about who I am as a person in anxious situations?
- What do I think other people think of me when I am in fear and anxiety?

The above questions are primarily interested in getting you connected to your internal narratives when you are anxious.

- Once you are connected to the feelings and thoughts, then reflect on the earliest memory you have when you felt a similar feeling.

The point of this task is to remember what you told yourself, rather than reliving the painful memory. It's the story you told yourself about you and life, not what happened to you, that we are looking for.

- What did you read about the world and your place

in it, during this experience?
- What did this event teach you about who you are?

The purpose here is NOT to 'adult' this process.
You don't want to think what you should have thought in this experience, or what you think of it now as an adult. You will know you are in an adult perspective because of the words you use, e.g., trying to justify a parent or assess the situation. The point here is to feel what you felt as the younger you at this time. What did you tell yourself through this experience about:

- Being lovable
- Being worthy
- Belonging
- Being capable
- Being powerful
- What lessons did you learn about life?
- What did you do to cope?
- If the enemy was trying to counsel you in this time, what was he saying?
- What ungodly agreements did you make?

Are you ready to replace?

 "Jesus, I come to You and open my heart.
I invite You to come and turn the lights on and help me identify unhealthy beliefs. Amen."

1. Ask the Holy Spirit to help you see His truth.
2. Share with the Holy Spirit everything that was painful in that moment.
3. Prophetic imagination: I want you to imagine this experience was represented as a coat that you wear. How would you describe it? Take time to imagine the colour, how it feels on your body, and the material it is made of. Feel what it feels like to be wearing it. Then, when you are ready remove it, imagine handing it to Jesus.
4. Now take some time to repent for believing the lies—remember this is not condemnation, but a gift to be realigned with truth and life.
5. Imagine you could go back in time. What would you want to say to yourself? Or if you were your child, what would you want to say? Write it down.
6. Ask the Holy Spirit what He wants to say to you in this experience and write it down.
7. Prophetic imagination: Imagine Jesus had another coat that He wants you to put on that represents what He says about the situation and about you. Put it on and let your prophetic imagination show you what it looks like to be "clothed in Christ" (Galatians 3:27). What does it feel like, look like, and even smell like? Then when you are ready, hand that back to Jesus in your heart.

I want you now to see both pieces of clothing in a closet. You have a choice to make as to which of the two coats you want to wear moving forward. Changing beliefs is your choice to make. Yes, Jesus has a new way, but you have to decide to put it on. You have to decide to wear Christ moving forward and not the old belief.

When you have made the decision, then get to work.

1. Ask Jesus if there is anyone you need to forgive and go through that process.
2. Break off any demonic attachments and agreements.
3. Ask Jesus to come and fill you afresh with all His love and truth.
4. Write down what you are choosing to believe as truth about you and your life moving forward. Put it on your phone or on your wall and repeat until it is second-hand nature.

HIGHLIGHTS

- This is a very important chapter to read and even more important to work through. I encourage you to grab a coffee, pen, and journal, head back to the start of the chapter, and let's go deep.

chapter 15

the ultimate comeback

Even the darkest night will end, and the sun will rise again.

Here we are at the conclusion of this journey together, and what a journey you've been on to arrive here. Let me just say, "Well done!" It has not been an easy road to incorporate new tools, grow in your maturity, and accept your level of personal responsibility in the healing process. I particularly want to commend you on the courage it took to set out to go deeper into painful moments in your life and invite Jesus in.

Go Jesus! Go you!

Let's have a bit of a recap of the terrain we have travelled. We started with the need of surrendering afresh to Jesus. The importance of this decision can never be understated. Whatever stage we find ourselves in along our walks of faith, living a life of surrender and then re-surrender to Jesus will always be a catalyst for transformation (as well as being the template for successful Christian living).

Then I shared around how anxiety works, the mechanics of it. How the *Flow of Stress*, can become a *Cycle of Anxiety*. The premise of this book was then stated: we want to deactivate that cycle. I demonstrated the theory of the *Storehouse of the Mind* and introduced the ideas of *Pleasure* and *Protect*. The hope of this was to show you that we can deactivate cycles of harmful and debilitating *Protect* by injecting *Pleasure*.

We looked at how we could inject *Pleasure*-inducing chemicals into the mind and soul. Gratitude, mindfulness, and self-care were all presented as power tools for deactivating anxiety. We then turned the corner in the journey to a spiritual spring clean. What does it mean to distinguish between God and the devil? What are the ways we give the devil access or agree with him, and how do we walk in authority? These were just some of the questions we examined.

As a Christian Minister, I guess this is both my grace zone and a large motivator for this book. Many books have been, and will be, written from a secular point of view on how we manage anxiety, and I encourage you to read them. I however wanted to offer some thoughts from a Christian perspective, which includes the spiritual realm. This was not for the faint hearted, so again, well done.

Finally, we brought all the tools together, and I showed you how they all are necessary in order to create lasting change. To deal with the deeper places of who you are and to allow Jesus into the depths of your life requires all these tools. Going to the core of our souls with Jesus is not a road everyone will travel. It is a rocky and difficult landscape to navigate. Like a strangle vine being pulled away from a maintained tree, the process can be one that is done tendril by tendril.

Of all the intentions I have had in writing this book, the most important has been to restore your hope for a better tomorrow. To offer a road map that empowers you with a sense of possibility around living the life you long for has been my greatest prayer.

As I think back over the last 20 years of my life, I can see panic attacks were my constant companion. Every major life event carried with it an assault of fear. Birthday parties, engagement parties, my wedding, baby showers, and every other event I have attended up until my forties, all have aspects of blurred memories due to anxiety attacks.

In my darkest times, I can only point you to Jesus in Gethsemane as the place I found solace. The dark night of the soul is desperately lonely, confronting, and exposing. How grateful I am that Jesus went before me, so He could be with me in my hardest time. Today I look back on that season, and the last 30 years of an anxiety journey, and marvel at what He has done. Whether on the highest heights or in the deepest depths, our Saviour has shared in all human experience.

I no longer live a life of dread or anxiety but one that hums with thankfulness and joy.

The undercurrent of my heart now meditates with gratitude and praise. I am living with deep contentment—change is possible, and I am proof of it. It would be a lie to say I am without any anxiety, but it's no longer debilitating.

The trajectory of my anxiety management is only getting better and better. Today, hand on heart, I am living a life that many years ago, I could only have longed for. My friend, a new day is possible for you too.

Successfully deactivating anxiety is not the absence of anxiety but knowing it doesn't get the final say.

At the beginning of my journey out of deactivating anxiety, I had lost all hope. I had resigned myself to the knowledge that life would never be different, and that there was no healing for my anxiety. I remember chatting with my mum, and she shared her own battles with anxiety over the years. In this conversation, she said something to me that reawakened hope. She told me, "It's possible to have a different life, Larissa." In that one conversation, a lifeline was thrown to me.

That hope was part of my ultimate comeback.

the ultimate comeback

I love a good comeback story! Give me a movie that has the main character or team out of contention and yet find a way to get back on top, and you have me! In fact, I will pick footy teams, swimmers or tennis players based solely on who looks most likely to lose. If you know much about Australians, it is actually a big part of our culture. We love what we call the Aussie Battler or the underdog being part of a comeback.

The greatest comeback story in all of history must be that of Jesus Christ. Could there be any greater defeat than death on a cross? Hanging in humiliation and being abused by your enemy as you take your last breath, it must have seemed like all was lost.

On the day of His death, His disciples were immersed in absolute hopelessness. They had dreams, they had plans, and they were all crushed. They couldn't see a clear path forward, but that wasn't the end of the story though, was it? Not even close!

The Cross only made sense when the day of the resurrection came. There will come a day when your cross will make sense too.

Everything about being a Christian hinges on the resurrection. Our faith is underpinned by a belief in a God that brings dead things back to life. A God that takes the broken and brings healing. A God that takes life's ashes and turns them into something beautiful. He is the God that makes a way where there seems to be no way and makes rivers where there's only been wilderness. Jesus is the God of the resurrection, and He will resurrect even your deepest disappointment, if you continue to follow His lead.

> If the Spirit of him who raised Jesus from the dead dwells in you, he who raised Christ Jesus from the dead will also give life to your mortal bodies through his Spirit which dwells in you.
> —Romans 8:11 (ESV)

The Jesus that I've been talking about, the One that has been walking with us through this book, is the God of the ultimate comeback. His resurrected Spirit desires to bring you into abundant life. Not fear, not disorder, not harm, not anxiety, dread, or oppression but a pure and glorious life. My prayer is that this book has progressed you toward that end.

Life can be different moving forward then it has been in the past.

The kicker in all this, perhaps the purpose in our literal madness at times, is that Jesus not only wants to de-active life sucking anxiety for you or I, but He also wants to do the same for our families and communities. He has plans to heal us AND if we are willing, to allow our lives to be a witness to others of His ability to do the same for them.

I wonder who could be on the other side of your determination to walk with Jesus and deactivate your anxiety?

You see, I believe, as I have shared my story, that you too will get to tell your story of deactivating anxiety; a story that's already written in eternity about how Jesus led you over this great mountain in your life and onto new adventures. Your story will not just be a 'survival guide,' but a life-giving testimony of how God's grace met you, just as I hope this book has been for you. When that day comes, I'd love you to let me know all about it, because your comeback – is at hand. ☺

Until our paths cross again, may the God of all peace richly bless you and walk with you as you continue to deactivate anxiety and claim the life that He has won for you. He is capable of it—and you are worth it.

bonus: your resource section

Mental Health Resources

Places to get support in Australia[15]

Kids Help Line
Phone: 1800 551 800
Webchat: kidshelpline.com.au/get-help/webchat-counselling
For anyone 25 years or under. This is a free, private, and confidential service.

Lifeline
Phone: 13 11 14
Webchat: lifeline.org.au/get-help/online-services/crisis-chat
For all ages, this is a 24/7 support service and suicide prevention service. This is a free, private, and confidential service.

Headspace
Phone: 1800 650 890
Free online and telephone service that supports young people between 12–25 and their families.

---

[15] Please note: If you are outside of Australia, or you cannot access these resources, ask your GP or health provider about support in your local area.

Headspace Parent Line

Phone: 1800 650 890

Headspace has extended its phone line to support parents who are concerned about their children's mental health.

MensLine Australia

Phone: 1300 78 99 78

A telephone, online support, information, and referral service for men dealing with men's mental health, relationship & divorce, emotional well-being, social connection.

Acute Mental Health Access Line

QLD: 1300 642 255
NSW: 1800 011 511
ACT: 1800 629 354
VIC: 1300 659 467
SA: 13 14 65
NT: 1800 682 288
WA: 1300 555 788 (Metro)
    1800 676 822 (Peel)
    1800 552 002 (Country/Rurallink)
TAS: 1800 332 388

Connect with Larissa:

Join the community on Facebook in the group De Activate Anxiety.

Facebook: facebook.com/larissanaybrock
Instagram: instagram.com/larissademichiel/
Home: larissademichiel.com
Coaching: larissademichiel.com/about-coaching
Speaking: larissademichiel.com/speaking

Other Helpful Resources:

My guided Christian mediations
larissademichiel.com/resource

Smiling Minds App
This is a great app that walks you through other guided mindful exercises.

Further Reading

Peter Scazzero, *Emotionally Healthy Spirituality, It's Impossible To Be Spiritually Mature while remaining Spiritually immature.*

John Mark Comer, *Ruthless Elimination of Hurry, Staying Emotionally Healthy and Spiritually Alive in our Current Chaos.*

Dr Caroline Leaf, *Switch on Your Brain. The Key to Peak Happiness, Thinking, and Health.*

Dr Caroline Leaf, *Cleaning Up Your Mental Mess: 5 Simple, Scientifically Proven Steps to Reduce Anxiety, Stress, and Toxic Thinking.*

Kris Vallotton, *Spirit Wars: Winning the Invisible Battle Against Sin and the Enemy.*

J.R Greenberg, *Comprehensive Stress Management.*

Martin E. P. Seligman, *Flourish: A visionary new understanding of happiness and well-being.*

John Paul Jackson, *Needless Casualties of War.*

Bibliography

Leaf, Dr Caroline, *Cleaning Up Your Mental Mess: 5 Simple, Scientifically Proven Steps to Reduce Anxiety, Stress, and Toxic Thinking,* Grand Rapids, Michigan: Baker Books, 2021.

Greenberg, J.R, 2020. *Comprehensive stress management.* 10th ed. New York, NY: McGraw-Hill, 2008.

drleaf.com/about/toxic-thoughts

thesuppersprograms.org/content/fight-or-flight-vs-rest-and-digest

ashimaliving.com/how-gratitude-can-reduce-anxiety-and-depression/

makedapennycooke.com/antidote-to-fear/

health.harvard.edu/blog/mindfulness-meditation-may-ease-anxiety-mental-stress-201401086967

caltech.edu/about/news/microbes-help-produce-serotonin-gut-46495

psychologytoday.com/nz/blog/all-about-addiction/201805/6-easy-ways-cultivate-positive-thinking-today?amp

acknowledgments

This book has not been a one-woman adventure.

Firstly, I would like to thank Jodie Thelning who helped me through my darkest days. You often brought me rays of light and wisdom. I remember one day chatting with you and you saying, "One day Larissa, this struggle will be used by God to help others". I hope that this book is just that.

Thank you to my previous Senior Pastor, Brad Bonhomme. You sparked the entire idea and name for this book. In about 2017, we had a conversation specifically around Christian leaders and that a book like this was needed. Thank you for believing I had something to say—turns out I did.

I'd also like to thank Psychologist Yvette Roma who was willing to nut through this book to make sure it was going to be helpful for people and not hurtful. I really appreciate you taking the time to offer an expert perspective.

A heart-felt thank you must also be given to the amazing and talented Kelly Weitz for your genius ability to take the heart of this book and create the cover. You are a stand-out in your generation, and an absolute gem in my world.

To Rebecca and her team at Star Label Publishing, what a pleasure it has been to work with you. Thank you for taking this book on and helping it to be brought to life—and to the shelves.

Mum, thank you for giving up almost a year of your life to care for us when I couldn't. Thank you also for reading over this manuscript, giving it your critical eye, and helping the work stay true to who I am.

To my two greatest friends, Kristy and Mel. Kristy, you are the greatest friend and ministry running mate I could ever have hoped for. You have been a friend through the seasons and championed me despite my hurdles. Mel, you have seen me in my darkest hours and remained convinced I would come out the other side to help others.

Lorenzo, you always believed this day would come. Thank you for listening to my 1000 daily ideas, for creating space in the diary for me to write and for letting me find my wings. You are a genuine man with a big heart and big belief in me. I love and appreciate you deeply.

Finally, to the One who loved me first, my heart is Yours. I pray I do justice to Your loving nature and healing power. My hope Jesus is that this book can reflect to those struggling with anxiety the same light on a path that You have given to me.

about the author

Larissa has an infectious passion for life that comes through in her down to earth, Australian style. She is an itinerate minister, published author and coach.

Larissa also has 20 years of secular coaching experience, a Bachelor in Theology, and served on the Governing board of Alphacrucis.

Larissa has been in Church leadership since 2000 and was on the pastoral team at Horizon Church from 2006-2020.

In 2021, along with her favourite people (her husband and two young girls), Larissa followed the call of God to start a new adventure on the Tweed Coast, NSW... and loving it!

Connect with Larissa
   Join the community – Facebook group
      @ De Activate Anxiety

   🌐 Larissademichiel.com
   f Facebook - Larissa De Michiel
   📷 Instagram - Larissa De Michiel

www.ingramcontent.com/pod-product-compliance
Lightning Source LLC
Chambersburg PA
CBHW070252010526
44107CB00056B/2434